© 2024 SENDCO Solutions All rights reserved.

Copyright Notice

This booklet is intended solely for use by the purchaser within their current institution. The material contained herein is protected by copyright law and may not be reproduced, distributed, or transmitted in any form or by any means, including photocopying, recording, or other electronic or mechanical methods, without the prior written permission of the publisher, except in the case of brief quotations embodied in critical reviews and certain other non-commercial uses permitted by copyright law.

Usage Restriction

This booklet has been written for use during the academic years 2024-2026. Due to the nature of educational change the author makes no assumptions that the content will still be relevant beyond this (!) Access to this material is restricted to the institution associated with the purchase. The purchaser may share the content with teachers and other staff employed by their associated institution for the purposes of training only.

Disclaimer

Every effort has been made to ensure the accuracy and completeness of the information contained in this book. However, the publisher, author, and contributors assume no responsibility for errors, omissions, or any consequences arising from the application of the information contained herein.

For permissions or further information, please contact:

enquiries@sendcosolutions.co.uk

www.sendcosolutions.co.uk

Images used in this booklet are provided by Widgit Symbols: Widgit Symbols © Widgit Software Ltd 2002 – 2024

CONTENTS

THE QFT SERIES 7

INTRODUCTION 9
    UNDERSTANDING QUALITY FIRST TEACHING 9
        Importance for SEN Students 9
        Goals and Objectives 10

CHAPTER 2: DEFINING TEACHER TALK 11
    DEFINING TEACHER TALK 11
        Key Aspects of Teacher Talk 11
        Impact of Teacher Talk on Learning Outcomes 11
        Effective Strategies 12
        Broader Impacts of Teacher Talk 13
    BENEFITS OF EFFECTIVE TEACHER TALK FOR SEN STUDENTS 14
        Examples of Effective Teacher Talk for SEN Students 15
        Research Insights 15
    COMMON CHALLENGES AND MISCONCEPTIONS 17
    REASONS FOR TEACHER TALK 19
        Providing Instructions 19
        Offering Feedback 19
        Classroom Management 19
        Engaging Students through Questioning 20
    RATIOS OF TEACHER TALK, STUDENT TALK, AND SILENCE 21
        The Balance of Teacher Talk 21
        The Importance of Student Talk 21
        The Role of Silence 22
        Varying Talk Dynamics Based on Activities 22
        Research Insights 22

CHAPTER 2: TEACHER TALK TECHNIQUES 24
    INTRODUCTION TO EFFECTIVE TEACHER TALK TECHNIQUES 24
    SIMPLIFY LANGUAGE 25
        Importance of Simplification 25
        Making Content Accessible for All Students 25
        Strategies for Simplifying Language Without Losing Content 26
        Practical Example 28
    CHECK FOR UNDERSTANDING 30
        The Purpose of Checking for Understanding 30

- *Ensuring Student Comprehension* *30*
- *Identifying Misunderstandings Early* *30*
- *Techniques for Effective Checking* *30*
- *Practical Example* *32*

REPETITION: REINFORCING LEARNING 34
- *When and How to Use Repetition* *34*
- *Identifying Key Concepts for Repetition* *34*
- *Examples and Best Practices for Repetition* *34*
- *Practical Examples in Different Subjects* *35*
- *Role of a Teaching Assistant:* *35*
- *Practical Example for Teacher Talk:* *36*

BROKEN RECORD TECHNIQUE: MAINTAINING FOCUS 37
- *Understanding the Broken Record Technique* *37*
- *Concept and Benefits:* *37*
- *Implementing the Broken Record Technique* *37*
- *Role of a Teaching Assistant:* *38*
- *Case Studies and Scenarios* *38*

VISUAL SUPPORT: ENHANCING COMPREHENSION 40
- *Types of Visual Supports* *40*
- *Integrating Visuals into Lessons* *41*
- *Examples of Effective Visual Supports* *41*
- *Practical Example for Teacher Talk* *42*

RECASTING: CORRECTING AND EXPANDING RESPONSES 44
- *What is Recasting?* *44*
- *Definition and Purpose:* *44*
- *Effective Recasting Techniques* *44*
- *Methods for Correcting and Expanding Student Responses:* *44*
- *Practical Applications in the Classroom* *45*
- *The latter two here being examples of correcting factual information.* *45*
- *Practical Example for Teacher Talk:* *45*
- *Differentiating Between Recasting, Repetition, and the Broken Record Technique* *46*

THINK-PAIR-SHARE 47
- *Description and Benefits* *47*
- *Enhancing Student Interaction and Learning* *47*
- *Implementation Strategies* *48*
- *Role of a Teaching Assistant in Think-Pair-Share* *48*
- *Practical Example for Teacher Talk* *49*

KAGAN STTRUCTURES 50
- *Description and Benefits* *50*
- *Common Kagan Structures* *50*

    Implementation Strategies 51
FRAYER MODELS 52
    Using Frayer Models for Concept Development 52
    Structure and Benefits: 52
    Practical Applications in the Classroom 52
    Examples and Best Practices 53
SENTENCE STARTERS 55
    Providing Scaffolds for Student Responses 55
    Importance of Sentence Starters 55
    Examples and Best Practices 55
    Effective Use in Different Subjects 57
PROVIDING CONSTRUCTIVE FEEDBACK 59
    Effective Feedback Methods 59
    Encouraging Student Reflection 60
SUMMARISING KEY TECHNIQUES 62
    Emphasising the Importance of Adaptation and Flexibility in Teaching 63

CHAPTER 3: QUESTIONING IN THE CLASSROOM 64

THE IMPORTANCE OF EFFECTIVE QUESTIONING 64
TYPES OF QUESTIONS: OPEN VS. CLOSED 66
    Definitions and Differences 66
    When to Use Open Questions 66
    When to Use Closed Questions 67
    Practical Application of Open and Closed Questions 67
BLOOM'S TAXONOMY AND QUESTIONING 70
    Overview of Bloom's Taxonomy 70
    Applying Bloom's Taxonomy to Questioning 70
    Encouraging Deeper Understanding for More and Most Able Students 71
    Examples of Questions at Different Levels 72
    Using Bloom's Taxonomy in Questioning 72
APPROACHES TO QUESTIONING FOR SEN STUDENTS 74
    Students with Autism (ASD/ASC) 74
    Students with Dyslexia 75
    Students with Attention Deficit Hyperactivity Disorder (ADHD) 75
    Students with Anxiety 75
    Students with Speech and Language Needs 76
    Students with Hearing Impairments 76
    Students with Cognitive Needs 76

CHAPTER 4: QUESTIONING STRATEGIES 78

- Introduction 78
- Differentiated Questioning Techniques 79
  - Understanding Differentiation 79
  - Strategies for Differentiated Questioning 79
- Tailoring Questions to Individual Needs 82
  - Assessing Student Needs 82
  - Adapting Questions for Different Abilities 82
  - Specific Techniques for Tailoring Questions 84
  - Tailoring Techniques to Specific Groups 86
- Scaffolding Questions for SEN Students 88
  - Importance of Scaffolding 88
  - Techniques for Effective Scaffolding 88
  - Using Visual Aids 89
  - Practical Examples of Scaffolding Questions 90
- Using Wait Time Effectively 92
  - Importance of Wait Time 92
  - Strategies for Implementing Wait Time 92
  - In the classroom 93
- Enhancing Engagement through Questioning 95
  - Encouraging Student Participation 95
  - Creating an Inclusive Environment 95
  - Building Confidence in Answering Questions 95
  - Strategies to Build Confidence: 96
  - Supporting Reluctant Responders 96
  - Identifying Reluctant Responders: 96
  - Strategies for Engaging Reluctant Responders: 96
- Assessment and Feedback through Questioning 98
  - Formative Assessment Techniques 98
  - Adapting Instruction Based on Responses 99
- Summarising Key Techniques in Questioning 102
  - Emphasising the Importance of Adaptation and Flexibility in Teaching 103
- 104

ABOUT THE AUTHOR 104

The QFT SERIES

In the ever-evolving landscape of education, ensuring that every child receives the support they need to thrive is paramount. The concept of Quality First Teaching (QFT) is at the heart of this mission, aiming to provide inclusive and high-quality education for all students. This series of booklets has been meticulously crafted to serve as a comprehensive guide for educators, particularly those working with Special Educational Needs (SEN) students.

Why These Booklets Have Been Written

The primary purpose of these booklets is to empower educators with practical strategies and insights into implementing QFT effectively in their classrooms. Each booklet addresses specific aspects of QFT, providing detailed guidance, real-world examples, and actionable steps to enhance teaching and learning experiences. Inclusion is not merely a policy but a practice that demands dedication, understanding, and continuous improvement. These booklets have been written to:

- Equip educators with the tools and knowledge to support students effectively.
- Foster an inclusive learning environment where every student feels valued and capable.
- Provide practical strategies that can be easily integrated into daily teaching practices.

List of Booklets in the Series

QFT 0 - Adaptive Teaching (publication August 2024)

QFT 1 - Scaffolding (publication August 2024)

QFT 2 - Teacher Talk and Questions (publication August 2024)

QFT 3 - Inclusive Classrooms (publication September 2024)

QFT 4 - Resources (publication October 2024)

QFT 5 - Reasonable Adjustments (publication November 2024)

QFT 6 - Technology (publication December 2024)

QFT 7 - Assessment (publication January 2025)

QFT 8 - Metacognition (publication February 2025)

QFT 9 - TA Support (publication March 2025)

QFT 10 - Instant Intervention (publication April 2025)

QFT 11 - Behaviour, Expectations and Engagement (publication May 2025)

Additional Resources:

- SENDCO Solutions offers engaging in-person or online training and support.
- SENsible SENCO has a video related to the content of this book.
- A printed version of this book is available to purchase from Amazon or the SENsible SENCO website.
- There is a set of Teacher/Trainer cards to support this content. Designed to be used individually in staff briefings or combined to make a longer training session, they provide a teacher cue card and trainer prompt. These are available from the SENsible SENCO website.

This book (QFT 2 – Teacher Talk and Questions) is supported by book 0 (Adaptive Teaching), Book 1 (Scaffolding), book 7 (Assessment) and book 8 (Metacognition).

INTRODUCTION

UNDERSTANDING QUALITY FIRST TEACHING

Quality First Teaching (QFT) is a comprehensive approach to education that ensures all students receive high-quality instruction from the outset. It involves employing effective teaching strategies that cater to the diverse needs of learners, fostering an inclusive environment where every student has the opportunity to succeed. QFT emphasises the importance of differentiated instruction, formative assessment, and creating a positive learning atmosphere.

Within the framework of QFT, teacher talk and questioning play pivotal roles. Effective teacher talk involves clear, concise communication that conveys information, instructions, and feedback in a way that is accessible to all students. Questioning, on the other hand, is a powerful tool for engaging students, assessing understanding, and promoting critical thinking. By strategically using questions, teachers can stimulate intellectual curiosity, guide learning, and provide immediate feedback.

Incorporating these elements into QFT ensures that teaching is not only about delivering content but also about actively involving students in the learning process. This dynamic interaction helps to create a classroom environment where students feel valued, supported, and motivated to learn.

Importance for SEN Students

Certain groups of students, such as those with Special Educational Needs (SEN), English as an Additional Language (EAL), and those from disadvantaged backgrounds (PP), require tailored approaches to teacher talk and questioning to meet their specific needs. These students often face unique challenges that can hinder their learning if not properly addressed.

- **SEN Students:** These students may struggle with cognitive processing, attention, and language comprehension. Effective teacher talk for SEN students involves simplifying language, using clear and consistent instructions, and providing scaffolding to support understanding. Questions should be adapted to their level of comprehension and include ample wait time to allow for processing.

- **EAL Students:** English language learners may face difficulties with vocabulary, grammar, and cultural nuances. Teachers can support EAL students by using visual aids, speaking slowly and clearly, and avoiding idiomatic expressions. Questions should be straightforward and supported with visual or contextual cues to aid understanding.

- **PP Students (Pupil Premium):** Students from disadvantaged backgrounds may lack access to resources and support outside of school. Effective teacher talk for PP students includes building a supportive classroom environment, using positive reinforcement, and providing explicit instructions. Questioning strategies should focus on building confidence and encouraging participation.

Adapting teacher talk and questioning techniques to meet the needs of these specific groups ensures that all students can engage with the material and achieve their full potential.

Goals and Objectives

The aim of this booklet is to provide educators with practical strategies and insights for enhancing their use of teacher talk and questioning in the classroom. By exploring various techniques and approaches, teachers can develop a toolkit that supports Quality First Teaching and meets the diverse needs of their students.

This booklet is designed to be flexible and user-friendly, allowing readers to dip in and out of chapters as needed. Each chapter focuses on a specific aspect of teacher talk and questioning, offering detailed explanations, practical examples, and real-world applications. Whether you are looking to refine your questioning techniques, better support SEN students, or enhance your overall communication skills, this booklet serves as a valuable resource.

Teachers are encouraged to approach the chapters in any order that makes sense for their individual needs and classroom contexts. By integrating the strategies discussed in this booklet, educators can create more inclusive, engaging, and effective learning environments that support the success of all students.

CHAPTER 2: DEFINING TEACHER TALK

DEFINING TEACHER TALK

Teacher talk refers to the verbal communication used by teachers to convey information, instructions, feedback, and manage classroom interactions. It encompasses all spoken exchanges between teachers and students during lessons, including explanations, questioning, praise, and discipline. Effective teacher talk is characterised by clarity, conciseness, and appropriateness for the age and developmental stage of the students.

Key Aspects of Teacher Talk

- Instructional Talk: This includes giving directions, explaining concepts, and providing necessary background information. Instructional talk aims to facilitate understanding and guide students through the learning process by modelling thought processes and cognitive strategies.

- Questioning: Teachers use questions to engage students, stimulate thinking, and check for understanding. Effective questioning techniques can encourage deeper learning and critical thinking, helping students articulate their reasoning and develop problem-solving skills.

- Feedback: Providing feedback on students' work and behaviour is crucial for learning and development. Feedback can be positive or constructive, helping students recognise their strengths and areas for improvement, thus motivating them and fostering a growth mindset.

- Classroom Management: This involves using verbal cues to manage classroom behaviour, establish routines, and create a conducive learning environment. Effective management also builds relationships and fosters a positive classroom culture.

Impact of Teacher Talk on Learning Outcomes

Research indicates that the quality and quantity of teacher talk significantly impact student learning outcomes. For instance, Hattie (2009) identifies teacher clarity as one of the most influential factors on student achievement, emphasising the importance of clear and effective communication in the classroom.

Teacher talk also plays a pivotal role in scaffolding student learning. Scaffolding, a concept introduced by Wood, Bruner, and Ross (1976), involves providing temporary support to students to help them achieve higher levels of understanding and skill. Through carefully structured teacher talk, educators can guide students through complex tasks, gradually reducing support as students become more competent.

Effective Strategies

Effective teacher talk strategies are essential for ensuring all students, including those with Special Educational Needs (SEN), can access and benefit from the educational content. One key strategy is simplification, which involves using language that is accessible to students without oversimplifying the content. This ensures that all students can follow along and understand the material, making the learning process more inclusive.

Another important strategy is repetition and reinforcement. By repeating key points and reinforcing important concepts, teachers can aid retention and help embed learning. This approach helps SEN students grasp and remember the material more effectively, as consistent repetition solidifies their understanding.

Checking for understanding is also a crucial aspect of effective teacher talk. Regularly asking questions and using formative assessment techniques allows teachers to gauge whether students comprehend the material. This continuous assessment ensures that any misunderstandings are promptly addressed, fostering a deeper understanding of the content.

Encouragement and motivation play a significant role in fostering a supportive and engaging learning environment. Using positive reinforcement to motivate and encourage student participation not only boosts students' confidence but also creates an atmosphere where they feel valued and supported. This approach is particularly beneficial for SEN students, who may require additional encouragement to participate actively in the classroom.

Incorporating these strategies into everyday classroom interactions can significantly enhance the effectiveness of teacher talk. Simplification ensures clarity, repetition and reinforcement aid retention, checking for understanding promotes comprehension, and encouragement fosters a positive and engaging learning environment. Together, these strategies help create an inclusive and supportive educational experience for all students, particularly those with SEN.

Broader Impacts of Teacher Talk

The impact of teacher talk extends beyond academic achievement; it also affects students' social and emotional development. According to Mercer and Dawes (2008), effective teacher talk fosters a positive classroom atmosphere, promotes respectful communication, and supports the development of social skills. This holistic approach helps create an inclusive and supportive learning environment where all students can thrive.

In summary, teacher talk is a fundamental component of classroom interaction, encompassing a range of verbal strategies aimed at enhancing student learning and development. Its effectiveness hinges on the teacher's ability to communicate clearly, engage students, provide appropriate feedback, and create a positive classroom environment.

BENEFITS OF EFFECTIVE TEACHER TALK FOR SEN STUDENTS

Effective teacher talk is essential in supporting students with Special Educational Needs (SEN), playing a crucial role in facilitating their learning, engagement, and development. When executed thoughtfully, teacher talk can significantly enhance the educational experience for SEN students.

One of the key benefits of effective teacher talk is enhanced comprehension and retention. Using clear and simplified language helps SEN students understand instructions and content more effectively. Breaking down complex ideas into manageable parts can significantly improve comprehension. Additionally, regularly repeating key points and reinforcing important concepts aids memory retention, making it easier for SEN students to grasp and remember the material.

Increased engagement and participation are also notable benefits of effective teacher talk. Engaging SEN students through targeted questions can stimulate their interest and encourage active participation. Asking open-ended questions allows students to express their thoughts and ideas, fostering a more interactive and inclusive classroom environment. Providing positive reinforcement and constructive feedback helps build confidence and motivation in SEN students. Recognising their efforts and achievements encourages continued participation and effort.

Improved social skills and behaviour are further benefits of effective teacher talk. Teacher talk serves as a model for appropriate social interactions and communication. By demonstrating respectful and effective communication, teachers help SEN students develop their own social skills. Using verbal cues to manage behaviour and establish routines provides structure and predictability, which is particularly beneficial for SEN students who may struggle with changes and disruptions.

Personalised learning and support are crucial for SEN students, and effective teacher talk plays a vital role in this area. Tailoring instructions to meet the specific needs of SEN students ensures they receive the appropriate level of support and challenge. Differentiated teacher talk addresses diverse learning styles and paces. Providing temporary support through structured teacher talk helps SEN students tackle complex tasks. Gradually reducing this support as students become more competent promotes independence and self-efficacy.

Effective teacher talk also fosters a positive learning environment. It helps create a sense of belonging and inclusivity by valuing and respecting each student's contributions. This supportive environment makes SEN students feel safe and encouraged to learn. Verbal encouragement and empathy from teachers help address the emotional and social needs of SEN students. A positive teacher-student relationship is essential for their overall well-being and academic success.

Examples of Effective Teacher Talk for SEN Students

Effective teacher talk involves using clear instructions, such as, "Please open your textbooks to page 34 and read the first paragraph. I'll explain any difficult words afterwards." This clarity helps SEN students know exactly what is expected of them. Reinforcement is another key element, illustrated by statements like, "Remember, we talked about this concept yesterday. Let's review it together before we move on." Such reinforcement aids in retaining information and connecting new learning to previous knowledge.

Encouragement is vital for building confidence in SEN students. For example, saying, "Great job, Sarah! You've made excellent progress on this problem," acknowledges their efforts and motivates them to continue. Behavioural cues also play a significant role in maintaining a conducive learning environment. An example would be, "I notice some of us are talking out of turn. Let's remember to raise our hands before speaking," which gently reminds students of expected behaviours.

In summary, effective teacher talk is a powerful tool in the inclusive classroom, providing enhanced comprehension, increased engagement, improved social skills, personalised support, and fostering a positive learning environment. By carefully crafting their verbal interactions, teachers can make a significant difference in the educational experiences of SEN students, supporting their academic and personal growth.

Research Insights

Studies highlight the profound impact of effective teacher talk on SEN students. For instance, research by Dockrell, Bakopoulou, Law, and Spencer (2012) found that teacher talk, which is clear, structured, and supportive, enhances the learning outcomes of students with speech, language, and communication needs (SLCN).

Furthermore, Dockrell and colleagues emphasised the importance of scaffolding and differentiated instruction to address individual needs.

Effective teacher talk is pivotal in supporting SEN students by enhancing comprehension, engagement, social skills, and personalised learning. By adopting clear, structured, and empathetic communication strategies, teachers can create an inclusive and supportive learning environment that fosters the academic and social development of SEN students.

COMMON CHALLENGES AND MISCONCEPTIONS

Implementing effective teacher talk in the classroom, particularly for students with Special Educational Needs (SEN), presents several challenges. Teachers often struggle to balance the clarity of their communication with the complexity required for deeper learning. Simplifying language too much can result in the loss of important content, while maintaining complexity can overwhelm SEN students. This delicate balance requires careful planning and thoughtful execution.

Managing classroom dynamics adds another layer of complexity. Differentiating teacher talk to address the diverse needs of students without singling out those with SEN can be challenging. Teachers must ensure their instructions and feedback are accessible to all students, fostering an inclusive learning environment.

Time constraints also pose a significant challenge. The pressure to cover curriculum content within limited timeframes can restrict opportunities for detailed explanations, repeated instructions, and personalised feedback, which are crucial for SEN students' understanding and retention of material. Additionally, managing emotional and behavioural issues that SEN students may exhibit can disrupt the flow of teacher talk, making effective communication even more challenging.

Another critical factor is the level of training and professional development that teachers receive. Many educators lack sufficient training in specialised communication strategies tailored for SEN students. While continuous professional development is essential, it is often inadequately prioritised, leaving teachers without the necessary tools to communicate effectively with all their students.

Several misconceptions about teacher talk further complicate its effective implementation. One common misconception is that more teacher talk equates to better learning outcomes. In reality, excessive teacher talk can overwhelm students and reduce opportunities for active engagement and learning. Quality, rather than quantity, is what drives effective teacher talk.

Another misconception is that simplifying language for SEN students means oversimplifying content. Effective teacher talk involves simplifying language thoughtfully, ensuring that content integrity is maintained while making it accessible. Additionally, not all feedback is constructive. Generic or overly critical feedback can demotivate students. Constructive feedback should be specific, positive, and focused on improvement.

There is also a misunderstanding that questioning is solely for assessing student understanding. Effective questioning stimulates thinking, encourages discussion, and models cognitive processes, making it a critical component of teacher talk. Finally, some educators view teacher talk as a one-way delivery of information. However, effective teacher talk is interactive, involving active listening, dialogue, and student participation.

To overcome these challenges and misconceptions, teachers can adopt several strategies. Balancing clarity with complexity can be achieved by using clear and concise language while incorporating key terms and concepts. Scaffolding learning by breaking down complex information into manageable parts can help maintain this balance.

Managing classroom dynamics involves employing differentiated instruction techniques to cater to diverse learning needs and using inclusive language that benefits all students. Addressing time constraints requires prioritising key concepts and integrating formative assessments into regular teaching to gauge understanding efficiently.

Handling emotional and behavioural issues involves developing classroom management strategies that include clear behavioural expectations and positive reinforcement, creating a supportive and predictable environment. Ongoing professional development focused on inclusive teaching strategies and effective communication with SEN students is crucial. Collaborating with special education professionals can enhance understanding and implementation of effective teacher talk.

Reframing misconceptions about teacher talk involves understanding that its quality is more important than its quantity, encouraging active learning and student participation. Simplifying language thoughtfully to maintain content integrity is essential, as is providing constructive, specific, and positive feedback tailored to individual student needs. Using questioning not only for assessment but also to stimulate thinking and dialogue, and fostering interactive communication that involves active listening and student engagement, are key components of effective teacher talk.

Addressing the challenges and misconceptions surrounding teacher talk is crucial for creating an effective and inclusive learning environment. By understanding these challenges and reframing misconceptions, educators can enhance their communication strategies, thereby better supporting the diverse needs of SEN students. Effective teacher talk is not just about conveying information but about fostering a supportive, engaging, and inclusive classroom atmosphere that promotes learning and development for all students.

REASONS FOR TEACHER TALK

Teacher talk is a fundamental component of classroom interaction, serving various crucial purposes that support effective teaching and learning. The primary purposes of teacher talk include providing instructions, offering feedback, managing the classroom, and engaging students through questioning. Each of these purposes plays a vital role in fostering a productive and inclusive learning environment, particularly for students with Special Educational Needs (SEN).

Providing Instructions

One of the primary reasons for teacher talk is to provide clear and concise instructions. Instructions guide students through tasks, ensuring they understand what is expected of them. Effective instructional talk sets the stage for learning by outlining steps, clarifying expectations, and providing necessary context. According to Hattie (2009), teacher clarity, which includes giving clear instructions, is one of the most influential factors on student achievement. Clear instructions help students focus on the task at hand, reducing misunderstandings and increasing efficiency and learning outcomes.

Offering Feedback

Feedback is another critical function of teacher talk. Providing timely and specific feedback helps students understand their progress, recognise their strengths, and identify areas for improvement. Feedback can be both encouraging and constructive, motivating students and fostering a growth mindset. Positive reinforcement builds confidence, while constructive feedback guides students on how to enhance their skills and knowledge. Research by Black and Wiliam (1998) emphasises the importance of formative feedback in promoting student learning and development. Effective feedback strategies help create a supportive learning environment where students feel valued and understood.

Classroom Management

Effective teacher talk is essential for classroom management. Teachers use verbal cues and clear communication to build relationships, establish routines, manage behaviour, and create an orderly environment conducive to learning. Setting clear expectations and consistently reinforcing them helps maintain a productive classroom atmosphere. Marzano, Marzano, and Pickering (2003) highlight the significance of effective classroom management in promoting student engagement and minimising disruptions. Teacher talk plays a vital role in implementing behaviour management strategies, ensuring that students understand and adhere to classroom norms and expectations.

Engaging Students through Questioning

Questioning is a powerful tool in the teacher's repertoire. Effective questioning techniques engage students, stimulate critical thinking, and check for understanding. Questions can be used to encourage students to articulate their thoughts, explore ideas, and engage in meaningful discussions. Open-ended questions, in particular, promote deeper learning by allowing students to express their reasoning and consider multiple perspectives. Research by Chin (2007) indicates that effective questioning techniques can significantly enhance students' cognitive engagement and learning outcomes. By varying the types of questions and incorporating strategies like wait time, teachers can create an interactive and inclusive classroom environment.

Teacher talk serves multiple essential functions in the classroom, from providing instructions and feedback to managing the classroom and engaging students through questioning. Each of these functions contributes to creating a supportive and effective learning environment. By understanding and effectively utilising these aspects of teacher talk, educators can better support all students, particularly those with SEN, fostering their academic and social development.

RATIOS OF TEACHER TALK, STUDENT TALK, AND SILENCE

Understanding the balance between teacher talk, student talk, and periods of silence is essential for creating an effective and engaging learning environment. Each element plays a distinct role in the educational process, and their proportions can significantly influence student outcomes.

The Balance of Teacher Talk

Teacher talk is a critical component of classroom interaction, necessary for providing instructions, delivering content, managing the classroom, and offering feedback. Research suggests that teacher talk should occupy approximately 30-50% of class time. Within this range, teachers can effectively cover key content, provide necessary explanations, and guide students through learning activities. Clarity and conciseness are crucial in teacher talk, ensuring that students understand instructions and content without feeling overwhelmed. Each instance of teacher talk should have a clear purpose, whether it's explaining a concept, giving instructions, or providing feedback. Moreover, engaging and interactive teacher talk can involve students more actively in the learning process through questioning and discussion.

The Importance of Student Talk

Student talk is equally important, ideally making up 30-50% of class time. This type of interaction is essential for active learning, allowing students to articulate their thoughts, engage in discussions, ask questions, and collaborate with peers. Through student talk, learners process information more deeply, develop critical thinking skills, and practice social interactions. Discussing and explaining concepts to peers helps students solidify their understanding and identify gaps in their knowledge. Engaging in dialogue encourages students to think critically and consider different perspectives. Additionally, collaborative activities and discussions foster communication skills and teamwork, essential for overall student development.

The Role of Silence

Silence, accounting for approximately 20% of class time, plays a critical role in the learning process. Often undervalued, periods of silence provide students with time to process information, reflect on what they have learned, and formulate their thoughts before responding or engaging in further activities. Silence allows students to reflect on their learning, making connections and deepening their understanding. It provides essential time for processing new information and integrating it with existing knowledge. Furthermore, silent periods give students the opportunity to formulate questions, responses, and ideas, enhancing their overall learning experience.

Varying Talk Dynamics Based on Activities

The dynamics of teacher talk, student talk, and silence can vary depending on the type of classroom activity. For instance, during the introduction of new material, increased teacher talk is necessary to set the context and explain new concepts. During class discussions, student talk should dominate as students share their thoughts, ask questions, and engage with the material and each other. In contrast, project work often involves increased periods of silence, allowing students time to work independently, reflect, and formulate their ideas. This balance ensures that students receive the necessary guidance and support from their teachers while also having ample opportunities to engage actively and reflectively with the content.

Research Insights

Several key studies and theories highlight the importance of balancing teacher talk, student talk, and silence. Lemke (1990) emphasises the importance of creating an interactive learning environment by balancing teacher and student talk. Fisher and Frey (2014) discuss the effectiveness of structured talk strategies in promoting student engagement and understanding. Rowe (1986) underscores the significance of wait time, demonstrating that giving students time to think before responding leads to more thoughtful and in-depth answers. These insights underline the need for educators to carefully manage the dynamics of classroom talk to enhance student learning outcomes.

Balancing teacher talk, student talk, and silence is essential for fostering an effective learning environment. Teacher talk is crucial for delivering content and guiding students, while student talk encourages active learning and critical thinking. Silence provides necessary reflection and processing time. By understanding and managing these dynamics, educators can create a more engaging and inclusive classroom that supports all students, particularly those with Special Educational Needs (SEN).

CHAPTER 2: TEACHER TALK TECHNIQUES

INTRODUCTION TO EFFECTIVE TEACHER TALK TECHNIQUES

In the previous chapters, we explored the value of teacher talk in the classroom, its impact on student learning, and the balance required between teacher talk, student talk, and silence. Building on this foundation, this chapter focuses on specific techniques that teachers can employ to make their verbal interactions more effective and supportive for all students, especially those with Special Educational Needs (SEN).

This chapter delves into practical strategies for simplifying language, checking for understanding, and using repetition to reinforce learning. It also explores techniques such as the Broken Record Technique for maintaining focus, visual supports for enhancing comprehension, and recasting for correcting and expanding student responses. Additionally, we will cover collaborative strategies like Think-Pair-Share, tools like Frayer Models, and the use of sentence starters to scaffold student responses. Finally, we will discuss the importance of preparation and planning in effective teacher talk.

By mastering these techniques, teachers can create a more inclusive, engaging, and productive learning environment, helping all students to achieve their full potential.

SIMPLIFY LANGUAGE

Importance of Simplification

Simplifying language is a crucial aspect of effective teacher talk, particularly in classrooms with diverse learners, including those with Special Educational Needs (SEN). Simplification helps ensure that all students can access and understand the instructional content. When teachers use clear and straightforward language, they reduce cognitive load, allowing students to focus on the core concepts rather than getting bogged down by complex vocabulary or convoluted sentence structures.

In UK classrooms, where inclusivity is a priority, simplifying language aligns with the principles of Universal Design for Learning (UDL). UDL advocates for instructional practices that accommodate all learners, providing multiple means of representation, engagement, and expression. Simplified language supports these principles by making content more accessible to students with varying language proficiencies, learning disabilities, or cognitive challenges.

Research supports the effectiveness of simplified language in enhancing comprehension and retention. For instance, studies by Sweller (1988) on cognitive load theory suggest that reducing unnecessary complexity in instructional materials helps students learn more effectively by allowing them to allocate their cognitive resources to understanding and processing essential information.

It's really important to remember carrier language and subject-specific terminology. Being mindful of common words that have different meanings across subjects. Carrier language refers to the simple, consistent language used to help convey complex ideas. It acts as a scaffold, supporting students' understanding of new concepts.

Making Content Accessible for All Students

Using simple and clear vocabulary is vital in ensuring that all students can grasp the material being taught. By avoiding jargon and unnecessary complexity, teachers can make learning more inclusive and effective.

Strategies for Simplifying Language Without Losing Content

Use Clear and Direct Vocabulary

Avoid Jargon and Technical Terms: When possible, use common words that students are likely to understand. If technical terms are necessary, provide clear definitions and use them consistently.

Select High-Frequency Words: Choose words that students encounter frequently in everyday language to help them connect new information with their existing knowledge base.

Break Down Complex Ideas

Chunk Information: Divide complex information into smaller, manageable "chunks." Present one idea at a time to avoid overwhelming students.

Use Short Sentences: Shorter sentences are easier to process. Aim to keep sentences concise and to the point, focusing on one main idea per sentence.

Employ Visual Aids

Incorporate Diagrams and Charts: Visual aids can help illustrate complex concepts, making them easier to understand.

Use Pictures and Symbols: Visual representations can support language comprehension, particularly for SEN students or those learning English as an additional language (EAL).

Utilise Repetition and Reinforcement

Repeat Key Points: Reinforce important concepts by repeating them in different ways. Use synonyms or rephrase key points to reinforce understanding.

Summarise Information: Provide brief summaries of the key points at the end of an explanation or lesson segment.

Check for Understanding

Ask Clarifying Questions: Use questions to check whether students understand the material. Encourage them to paraphrase what they have learned.

Provide Immediate Feedback: Offer prompt feedback to correct misunderstandings and reinforce correct responses.

Carrier Language

Definition and Importance: Carrier language consists of straightforward, familiar phrases and words used to introduce and explain new content. This language serves as a bridge, helping students grasp complex ideas by connecting them with concepts they already know.

Examples: Phrases like "This means that..." or "In other words..." help clarify explanations and make new information more accessible.

Common Words with Different Meanings

Subject-Specific Terminology: Some common words have different meanings depending on the subject area, which can confuse students. For example, the word "mean" has a specific definition in mathematics (average value) and a different one in English (to signify or intend).

Strategies to Address Confusion: When introducing such terms, explicitly teach the different meanings and provide context. Use visual aids or examples to illustrate how the word's meaning changes depending on the subject.

Use Examples and Analogies

Relate to Everyday Experiences: Use examples from students' daily lives to explain abstract concepts. Analogies can help bridge the gap between familiar and new ideas.

Contextualise New Information: Place new information in a context that is relevant and meaningful to the students, helping them see its application and importance.

Implement Scaffolded Support

Gradual Release of Responsibility: Start with more guided instruction and gradually allow students to take on more responsibility as they become more comfortable with the material.

Provide Step-by-Step Instructions: For complex tasks, provide detailed steps and check for understanding at each stage.

Employ Visual Support Tools

Mind Maps and Graphic Organisers: These tools help students visually organise information, making it easier to understand relationships and hierarchies within the content.

Colour Coding and Highlighting: Use colours to highlight key information or differentiate between different types of information.

Practical Example

When teaching a complex concept like photosynthesis in a primary school classroom, a teacher might use the following simplified approach:

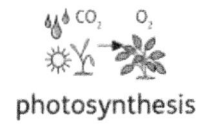

photosynthesis

1. Introduction:

    "Photosynthesis is how plants make their food. They use sunlight, water, and air."

2. Chunking Information:

    "First, plants take in sunlight. Then, they use water from the soil. Finally, they use a gas called carbon dioxide from the air."

3. Visual Aids:

    Show a diagram of a plant with arrows pointing to the sun, water in the soil, and carbon dioxide in the air.

4. Use of Repetition:

    "Remember, plants need three things to make food: sunlight, water, and carbon dioxide. Can anyone tell me the three things plants need?"

5. Checking for Understanding:

   Ask students to explain in their own words how plants make food.

By employing these strategies, teachers can make complex content accessible without diluting the essential information, ensuring that all students can engage with and understand the material.

CHECK FOR UNDERSTANDING

The Purpose of Checking for Understanding

Checking for understanding is a fundamental component of effective teaching. It ensures that students are not merely following along with the lesson but are genuinely comprehending the material being presented. This process helps identify any misconceptions or gaps in knowledge early, allowing for timely intervention and support. For teachers, it provides immediate feedback on the effectiveness of their instruction, enabling them to adjust their teaching strategies to meet the needs of their students.

In the UK, where classrooms are often diverse and inclusive, checking for understanding is particularly crucial. It ensures that all students, including those with Special Educational Needs (SEN), are keeping pace with the lesson. By actively monitoring comprehension, teachers can create a more inclusive learning environment where every student has the opportunity to succeed. Whilst there are many methods to check for understanding, this booklet focuses on those related to teacher talk.

Ensuring Student Comprehension

Ensuring that students understand the material is not only about checking but also about creating opportunities for students to demonstrate their knowledge. This involves using a variety of methods to make sure all students, regardless of their learning styles or abilities, can show what they have learned.

Identifying Misunderstandings Early

Early identification of misunderstandings allows teachers to address issues before they become ingrained. This proactive approach helps prevent gaps in knowledge from widening and supports continuous learning progress.

Techniques for Effective Checking

Clarifying Questions

Asking clarifying questions is an immediate way to check for understanding. These questions require students to explain concepts in their own words or to elaborate on their initial responses. This technique helps teachers gauge the depth of students' comprehension.

After explaining the concept of photosynthesis, a teacher might ask, "Can someone explain how sunlight is used in photosynthesis?" This requires students to recall and apply what they have learned, providing insight into their understanding.

Paraphrasing and Summarising

Encouraging students to paraphrase or summarise what they have just learned is another effective technique. This method checks their ability to process and articulate the information.

After a discussion on the causes of World War I, the teacher might say, "In your own words, summarise the main reasons why the war started." This encourages students to condense the information and present it clearly.

Think-Alouds

Think-alouds involve the teacher verbalising their thought process while working through a problem or concept. This technique models cognitive strategies and allows students to hear how an expert approaches a task, making their own thought processes more visible and understandable.

While solving a maths problem, the teacher might say, "First, I see that I need to find the value of x. I know I need to isolate x by subtracting 5 from both sides of the equation..." This helps students follow the logical steps involved.

Think-Pair-Share

Think-Pair-Share is a collaborative learning strategy that allows students to process and discuss their understanding before sharing it with the class. This technique promotes engagement and deeper comprehension through peer interaction.

After introducing a new science concept, the teacher asks students to think about a related question, discuss it with a partner, and then share their thoughts with the class. This sequence helps students articulate their understanding and learn from each other.

Summative Sentences

Summative sentences involve asking students to summarise the lesson in one or two sentences. This technique forces students to distill the essence of the lesson into its most critical points.

At the end of a lesson on the water cycle, the teacher might ask, "Can you summarise the water cycle in one sentence?" This encourages students to focus on the key components and their relationships.

Probing Questions

Probing questions delve deeper into students' understanding, requiring them to think critically and justify their answers. These questions often begin with "why" or "how."

After discussing the impact of climate change, a teacher might ask, "Why do you think reducing carbon emissions is important for the environment?" This encourages students to think beyond surface-level responses and explore underlying reasons.

Practical Example

To illustrate these techniques, consider a lesson on the water cycle in a primary school classroom:

1. Clarifying Questions:

   After explaining evaporation, the teacher asks, "Can someone explain what happens during evaporation in your own words?"

2. Paraphrasing and Summarising:

   Following a discussion on condensation, the teacher says, "Summarise how condensation contributes to the water cycle."

3. Think-Alouds:

    While describing precipitation, the teacher verbalises, "When clouds get heavy with water droplets, they release the water as rain. This is called precipitation."

4. Think-Pair-Share:

    Students are asked to think about where they have seen evaporation in their daily lives, discuss with a partner, and then share with the class.

5. Summative Sentences:

    At the end of the lesson, the teacher asks, "Can you summarise the entire water cycle in one sentence?"

6. Probing Questions:

    After discussing the water cycle, the teacher asks, "Why do you think the water cycle is essential for life on Earth?"

REPETITION: REINFORCING LEARNING

When and How to Use Repetition

Repetition is a powerful teaching strategy that reinforces learning and ensures students retain key concepts. When used effectively, it helps students remember information, understand complex ideas, and build confidence in their knowledge. Teachers should strategically incorporate repetition at various stages of the learning process.

Repetition is particularly useful when introducing new concepts. By repeating new information, teachers help embed it in students' long-term memory. This approach is also beneficial before assessments, as it reinforces key points, ensuring students recall essential information during tests. Additionally, repetition is invaluable when teaching difficult topics, as it aids comprehension and retention.

Cognitive science highlights the importance of repetition in combatting the forgetting curve, a concept developed by Hermann Ebbinghaus. The forgetting curve illustrates how information is lost over time when there is no attempt to retain it. Repetition, especially spaced repetition, helps reinforce learning and combat this natural decline in memory retention. By repeatedly exposing students to key concepts over spaced intervals, teachers can enhance long-term retention and reduce forgetting.

Identifying Key Concepts for Repetition

Not all content requires the same level of repetition. Teachers should focus on core concepts that are foundational to understanding a topic. These key concepts can be identified by aligning repetition with the learning objectives outlined in the curriculum, recognising areas where students frequently make mistakes, and highlighting information that serves as a foundation for more advanced topics.

Examples and Best Practices for Repetition

Integrating repetition naturally into teaching practice involves several effective strategies. Regular reviews at the beginning of lessons help reinforce previously covered material. After explaining a concept, summarising the main points and asking students to repeat them ensures comprehension. Posing questions that require students to recall and apply previously learned information also reinforces learning.

Rosenshine's Principles of Instruction emphasise the importance of repetition for effective teaching. According to Rosenshine, reviewing material frequently and providing ample practice opportunities are essential for helping students master new content. By revisiting previously taught material, teachers can ensure that students retain and build upon their knowledge, fostering deeper understanding and skill development.

Practical Examples in Different Subjects

Repetition can be effectively applied across various subjects. In maths, key concepts such as basic operations, formulas, and problem-solving strategies benefit from repeated use in different problems over several lessons. For example, after teaching a formula, teachers can repeatedly use it in various problems and ask students to explain the steps in their own words.

In science, repetition is essential for understanding scientific processes, terminology, and principles. For instance, when teaching the water cycle, teachers can repeatedly describe each stage—evaporation, condensation, and precipitation—using diagrams, discussions, and written summaries. This repeated exposure helps students retain and comprehend the process.

In English, grammar rules, vocabulary, and literary analysis techniques are key areas for repetition. Introducing new vocabulary words and using them repeatedly in different contexts ensures students understand and remember them. Encouraging students to write sentences and stories using the new vocabulary reinforces their learning.

In history, significant events, dates, and figures benefit from repetition. After discussing a historical event, teachers can ask students to summarise the causes and effects, revisiting these summaries in subsequent lessons to reinforce their understanding.

Role of a Teaching Assistant:

Teaching assistants (TAs) play a pivotal role in implementing repetition strategies effectively. They can support individual students or small groups by providing additional practice and reinforcing key concepts. For example, a TA might work with a group of students to review a math formula repeatedly, ensuring they understand and remember it. TAs can also use repetition in one-on-one settings to help students with special educational needs (SEN) or those learning English as an additional language (EAL) grasp and retain important information. By offering consistent, patient reinforcement, TAs help build students' confidence and mastery of the material.

Practical Example for Teacher Talk:

When teaching a complex concept like fractions in a primary school classroom, a teacher might use the following repetitive approach:

First, the teacher introduces the concept: "Today, we are learning about fractions. Fractions are parts of a whole." They then provide an initial explanation: "A fraction has two parts: the numerator (top number) and the denominator (bottom number)."

Using visual aids, such as a pie chart divided into equal parts, helps illustrate the concept, with the teacher highlighting the numerator and denominator. To reinforce this, the teacher repeats the explanation: "Remember, the numerator tells us how many parts we have, and the denominator tells us how many equal parts the whole is divided into."

The teacher then engages students in interactive repetition by asking, "If we have a pie divided into four parts and one part is eaten, what fraction of the pie is eaten?" This helps students apply the concept. The teacher reinforces this by summarising: "So, if one part out of four is eaten, the fraction is one-quarter."

Finally, to check for understanding, the teacher asks, "Who can tell me what the numerator and denominator represent in one-quarter?" This ensures that students grasp the concept and can articulate it.

BROKEN RECORD TECHNIQUE: MAINTAINING FOCUS

Understanding the Broken Record Technique

The broken record technique is a teaching strategy that involves repeating the same phrase or instruction multiple times, much like a broken record that keeps playing the same part of a song. This method is particularly beneficial for students with Speech, Language and Communication Needs (SLCN) or those learning English as an Additional Language (EAL). These students often require more time to process information and benefit from hearing the same words used consistently.

Concept and Benefits:

The primary concept behind the broken record technique is repetition, which reinforces understanding and helps maintain focus. By repeating instructions or key information in the same words, teachers provide students with multiple opportunities to process and internalise the message. This consistency is crucial for children with SLCN or EAL, as it reduces confusion and cognitive overload, allowing them to focus on comprehension rather than deciphering new vocabulary or phrasing each time.

The benefits of the broken record technique include:

- Enhanced Comprehension: Repetition helps solidify understanding by giving students extra processing time.

- Reduced Anxiety: Familiar phrases and instructions reduce the stress associated with trying to understand new or complex language.

- Increased Focus: Repetition helps maintain students' attention on the task at hand, especially for those who may be easily distracted or overwhelmed by too much information at once.

Implementing the Broken Record Technique

To effectively implement the broken record technique, teachers should follow a few key steps:

Steps for Effective Use:

1. Identify Key Phrases: Determine the essential instructions or information that students need to understand and repeat these consistently.

2. **Maintain Consistency:** Use the exact same wording each time you repeat the phrase. Avoid changing the wording, as this can confuse students.
3. **Pace the Repetition:** Allow students time to process each repetition. Don't rush through the repetitions; give them space to think and understand.
4. **Use Visual Supports:** Where possible, accompany the repeated phrases with visual aids to reinforce understanding.
5. **Check for Understanding:** Periodically ask students to repeat the phrase or instruction back to you to ensure they have grasped the concept.

Role of a Teaching Assistant:

Teaching assistants (TAs) are essential in the effective use of the broken record technique, especially for students with SLCN or EAL. TAs can provide consistent repetition of instructions or key information to ensure these students have ample time to process and understand. In small group settings or one-on-one sessions, TAs can use the exact same wording each time they repeat an instruction, reducing confusion and reinforcing comprehension. By working closely with individual students, TAs help maintain focus and ensure that everyone is keeping up with the lesson, thereby supporting a more inclusive learning environment.

Case Studies and Scenarios

Scenario 1: Giving Instructions in Maths In a primary school maths lesson, a teacher is explaining a new concept: adding fractions. The teacher uses the broken record technique to reinforce the steps.

Teacher: "To add fractions, you need the same denominator. First, find a common denominator. Can everyone say that with me? Find a common denominator."

The teacher repeats this phrase several times during the lesson. Students, especially those with SLCN or EAL, benefit from hearing the same instruction repeatedly, allowing them to focus on understanding the steps without getting lost in new vocabulary.

Scenario 2: Classroom Behaviour Management A teacher uses the broken record technique to manage classroom behaviour.

Teacher: "When you hear the bell, stop what you are doing and look at me. When you hear the bell, stop what you are doing and look at me."

By repeating this instruction consistently, students learn to associate the sound of the bell with the expected behaviour. This repetition helps all students, but especially those with SLCN or EAL, to understand and follow classroom routines.

Scenario 3: Science Experiment Instructions During a science experiment, a teacher provides instructions using the broken record technique.

Teacher: "Pour the liquid into the beaker, then stir. Pour the liquid into the beaker, then stir."

This clear, repeated instruction ensures that all students, including those who may need more time to process, understand exactly what they need to do. The teacher checks for understanding by asking a few students to repeat the instruction back.

VISUAL SUPPORT: ENHANCING COMPREHENSION

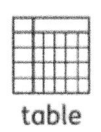

bar chart   venn diagram   table

Types of Visual Supports

Visual aids are powerful tools that can significantly enhance comprehension and retention of information. They provide students with concrete representations of abstract concepts, making it easier for them to understand and remember new material. The types of visual supports include charts, diagrams, graphs, pictures, and symbols. These aids are especially beneficial for many students with additional needs including those with Speech, Language and Communication Needs (SLCN), English as an Additional Language (EAL), or Dyslexia, as they offer an alternative way to process information.

pie chart

Charts organise information visually, making it easier to compare and contrast data. Examples include bar charts, pie charts, and flowcharts. Diagrams illustrate how things work or the relationships between different components, such as Venn diagrams, circuit diagrams, and process diagrams. Graphs present data in a visual format, helping students to see patterns and trends, with examples like line graphs, scatter plots, and histograms.

number line

Pictures and symbols can represent words or concepts, aiding in understanding and memory. This is particularly useful for younger students or those with limited language proficiency.

Integrating Visuals into Lessons

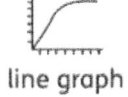

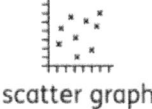

Integrating visual aids into lessons involves more than simply showing a picture or chart; it requires thoughtful planning to ensure that visuals effectively support the learning objectives. Teachers should choose visuals that directly relate to the key concepts of the lesson and ensure they are clear and not overly complex. Visuals should simplify the information, not complicate it. When using symbols or icons, keeping them consistent throughout the lesson avoids confusion. Encouraging students to interact with the visuals, such as by labelling diagrams or creating their own charts, also helps. Always accompany visual aids with clear verbal explanations. This dual coding approach (visual and verbal) enhances understanding and retention.

Examples of Effective Visual Supports

Visual aids can be effectively applied across various subjects. In maths, number lines help students understand addition, subtraction, and the concept of negative numbers. For instance, when teaching addition, a teacher can use a number line to show how to move right from a starting number. Diagrams of geometric shapes can help students visualise properties like angles, sides, and symmetry.

In science, diagrams showing the life cycle of a butterfly or frog help students understand biological processes.

periodic table

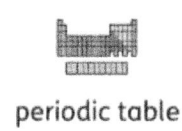

The periodic table is a visual tool that helps students learn about elements and their properties.

In English, story maps help students organise the elements of a story, such as setting, characters, plot, and resolution. Charts showing parts of speech or sentence structure can aid in understanding grammar rules.

timeline

In history, timelines provide a visual representation of historical events, helping students understand the sequence and context of occurrences. Maps are essential for teaching geography and historical events, helping students understand locations and movements.

picture   sketch   photo   drawing   symbol

Practical Example for Teacher Talk

In a school science lesson on plant growth, a teacher might use the following approach to integrate visual aids effectively:

roots

The lesson begins with an introduction using a visual aid: "Today, we are learning about how plants grow. Look at this diagram of a plant. Can you see the roots, stem, leaves, and flowers?" This sets the stage for the lesson, providing students with a clear visual reference.

stem

The teacher then explains each part of the plant using the diagram: "The roots take in water from the soil. The stem carries the water to the leaves. The leaves use sunlight to make food for the plant." This step-by-step explanation, supported by the visual diagram, helps students understand the function of each plant part.

leaves

Next, the teacher engages students with an interactive element: "Now, let's label the parts of the plant together. What is this part called?" (points to the roots). This interaction ensures that students are actively participating and reinforces their learning.

flowers

To reinforce the information, the teacher combines visuals with talk: "Remember, the roots, stem, leaves, and flowers all have important jobs. Can anyone tell me what the leaves do?" This repetition, supported by the visual aid, helps solidify the students' understanding.

Using Widgit symbols can further enhance this approach. For example, when discussing plant parts, using Widgit symbols for "roots," "stem," "leaves," and "flowers" can provide additional visual cues that reinforce learning.

RECASTING: CORRECTING AND EXPANDING RESPONSES

What is Recasting?

Recasting is an instructional technique used by teachers to correct and expand upon students' responses without directly pointing out errors. Instead of explicitly correcting a mistake, the teacher reformulates the student's response into a correct or more sophisticated version. This method is particularly effective in supporting language development and fostering a positive learning environment.

Definition and Purpose:

Recasting involves subtly correcting a student's error by rephrasing their response. The primary purpose is to model the correct form or a more advanced version of the response, which helps students learn from their mistakes without feeling discouraged. This technique promotes language development, enhances comprehension, and encourages students to communicate more effectively.

Effective Recasting Techniques

Effective recasting requires careful listening and the ability to provide immediate, constructive feedback. Teachers should aim to maintain a supportive and encouraging tone, ensuring that students feel valued and understood.

Methods for Correcting and Expanding Student Responses:

- Implicit Correction: Without highlighting the error, the teacher restates the student's response correctly. For example, if a student says, "He go to the store," the teacher might respond, "Yes, he goes to the store."

- Expansion: The teacher adds information to the student's response to make it more complete or sophisticated. If a student says, "The plant needs water," the teacher might say, "Yes, the plant needs water and sunlight to grow."

- Clarification Requests: The teacher asks for clarification, prompting the student to rethink and correct their own response. For instance, "Can you explain what you mean by 'he go'?"

- Restatement with Emphasis: The teacher repeats the student's response with emphasis on the correct form. If a student says, "She run fast," the teacher might reply, "Yes, she **runs** fast."

Practical Applications in the Classroom

Recasting can be applied across various subjects and grade levels, helping to correct misconceptions and expand student understanding in a non-threatening way.

Examples Across Different Subjects:

English: In an English lesson on sentence structure, a student might say, "She don't like apples." The teacher can recast this by saying, "She doesn't like apples. What fruits does she like?"

Maths: During a maths lesson on fractions, a student might say, "Two third is more than one half." The teacher could respond, "Actually, two-thirds is more than one-half. Can you show me why using a visual?"

Science: In a science lesson about the water cycle, a student might say, "Water evaporates from plants." The teacher can expand this by saying, "Yes, water evaporates from plants, which is called transpiration. Can you explain what happens next in the water cycle?"

History: During a history discussion about World War II, a student might say, "The war started in 1938." The teacher might recast this by saying, "Actually, the war started in 1939. What events led to the beginning of the war?"

The latter two here being examples of correcting factual information.

Practical Example for Teacher Talk:

In a primary school classroom discussing photosynthesis, a student might say, "The plant make food with sun." The teacher can use recasting to correct and expand the response: "Yes, the plant **makes** food with sunlight through a process called photosynthesis. Can anyone tell me what else the plant needs to make food?"

Differentiating Between Recasting, Repetition, and the Broken Record Technique

While recasting, repetition, and the broken record technique all involve repetition of information, they serve different purposes and are used in distinct ways.

- Repetition: This involves repeating key information multiple times to reinforce learning and ensure retention. It is particularly useful for embedding new concepts in students' long-term memory.

- Broken Record Technique: This method involves repeating the same instruction or phrase consistently, using the same words each time. It helps maintain focus and comprehension, especially for students who need extra processing time.

- Recasting: This technique involves subtly correcting and expanding a student's response by rephrasing it. It focuses on modelling correct language use and expanding student understanding without directly pointing out errors.

THINK-PAIR-SHARE

Description and Benefits

Think-Pair-Share is an interactive instructional strategy designed to enhance student engagement and learning through structured peer interaction. This technique involves three stages: first, students think individually about a question or problem; next, they pair up with a partner to discuss their thoughts; and finally, they share their ideas with the larger group.

The benefits of Think-Pair-Share are significant. It enhances comprehension by encouraging students to verbalise their thoughts and hear different perspectives, deepening their understanding of the material. This method increases participation, ensuring that all students, including those who might be reluctant to speak in front of the whole class, have a voice. It also improves communication skills, as students learn to articulate ideas clearly and listen actively to others. Furthermore, Think-Pair-Share fosters collaboration, promoting a learning environment where students work together and respect diverse viewpoints.

Enhancing Student Interaction and Learning

Think-Pair-Share enhances student interaction and learning by providing a structured yet flexible framework for discussion. During the "think" phase, students have the opportunity to process information individually, catering to those who need time to formulate their thoughts. The "pair" phase allows for meaningful peer interaction, where students can exchange ideas and challenge each other's thinking. Finally, the "share" phase brings the entire class into the discussion, fostering a sense of community and collective learning.

To implement Think-Pair-Share effectively, start by posing a thought-provoking question. This question should stimulate critical thinking and be relevant to the lesson's objectives. Open-ended questions work best as they encourage diverse responses. Give students a few minutes to think about the question individually, encouraging them to jot down their thoughts or notes to help organise their ideas.

Next, instruct students to pair up with a partner to discuss their thoughts. Provide clear guidelines on what to discuss and remind them to listen actively to their partner's ideas. After the pairs have had sufficient time to discuss, bring the class back together and ask pairs to share their insights with the larger group. Facilitate the discussion by summarising key points and encouraging further elaboration.

Implementation Strategies

For Think-Pair-Share to be effective, it should be thoughtfully integrated into the lesson plan and tailored to the specific needs of the class. Providing explicit instructions for each phase of the activity is crucial. Make sure students understand what they are expected to do during the think, pair, and share stages. Managing the time allocated to each phase carefully is also important. Allow enough time for meaningful discussion, but keep the activity within a reasonable timeframe to ensure it remains dynamic and engaging.

Consider how you pair students. Pairing students of different abilities can lead to more productive discussions, as higher-achieving students can help others grasp complex concepts. Alternatively, pairing students with similar abilities can encourage peer support and confidence-building. Actively monitor the pairs during the discussion phase by walking around the classroom, listening in on conversations, providing guidance, and ensuring all students are participating. After the share phase, provide feedback to the class on their discussions. Highlight insightful contributions and correct any misconceptions that may have arisen.

Role of a Teaching Assistant in Think-Pair-Share

Teaching assistants (TAs) play a crucial role in the successful implementation of Think-Pair-Share, particularly in supporting students who may need additional help. Here's how TAs can contribute:

- Facilitating Pairing: TAs can assist in pairing students thoughtfully, ensuring that each pair is productive and supportive. They can help match students with complementary skills or needs, fostering a balanced and effective learning environment.

- Supporting Individual Students: During the "think" phase, TAs can provide one-on-one support to students who might struggle to formulate their thoughts independently. They can ask guiding questions or provide prompts to help these students engage with the material.

- Monitoring Discussions: While the teacher oversees the entire class, TAs can focus on specific pairs, especially those that may need more support. They can ensure that discussions stay on track, encourage shy or reluctant students to participate, and help clarify any misunderstandings.

- Encouraging Participation: TAs can gently prompt students to share their ideas during the "share" phase, providing a confidence boost for those who might be hesitant to speak in front of the class. They can also help articulate ideas for students who have difficulty expressing themselves.

- Providing Feedback: After the activity, TAs can offer targeted feedback to students, reinforcing what was discussed and highlighting areas for improvement. This feedback can be particularly valuable for students with specific learning needs.

- Enhancing Inclusivity: By working closely with students who have special educational needs or those learning English as an additional language, TAs ensure that these students are fully included in the activity. They can adapt materials or provide extra explanations as needed.

Practical Example for Teacher Talk

In a primary school English lesson on character analysis, a teacher might use Think-Pair-Share to explore the motivations of a character in a story. The teacher begins by posing the question: "Why do you think the character decided to help the stranger, even though it was risky?" Students are given a few minutes to consider the question individually and write down their thoughts.

Next, students pair up and discuss their ideas. They are encouraged to consider their partner's perspective and think about how it relates to their own. Finally, the teacher brings the class back together and asks pairs to share their conclusions. The teacher facilitates a discussion by connecting different ideas and encouraging further analysis.

KAGAN STTRUCTURES

Description and Benefits

Kagan Structures are cooperative learning strategies designed to promote engagement, teamwork, and active participation among students. Developed by Dr. Spencer Kagan, these structures provide a framework for interaction that ensures equal participation and accountability, fostering a more inclusive and dynamic classroom environment.

Kagan Structures are characterised by simultaneous interaction, equal participation, positive interdependence, and individual accountability. These key features ensure that all students participate actively, share responsibility, and are accountable for their learning.

Common Kagan Structures

One of the most frequently used Kagan Structures is the Rally Robin, where students take turns responding orally to a question or prompt. This structure is excellent for brainstorming, review, and generating multiple responses. In practice, a teacher might pose a question and have students pair up, taking turns to share their responses and build upon each other's ideas. For example, in a history lesson, students might alternate listing causes of the Industrial Revolution, thus deepening their understanding through shared knowledge.

Another effective structure is Timed Pair Share, where students share with a partner for a predetermined amount of time. This technique promotes equal participation and helps students practice concise communication. A typical implementation involves providing a prompt and setting a timer, allowing one student to share before switching roles. In a language arts class, for instance, students might discuss their interpretations of a poem, refining their thoughts through focused dialogue.

The Round Robin structure ensures that each student in a small group takes turns sharing a response, fostering inclusivity and comprehensive engagement. Teachers might form small groups, pose a question, and have each student share their answer in turn. In a science class, students might take turns explaining steps in the scientific method, benefiting from varied explanations and perspectives.

Numbered Heads Together is another popular structure where students are grouped and given numbers. The teacher poses a question, groups discuss the answer, and one student from each group is randomly selected to share. This method ensures that all students are prepared to contribute, promoting accountability and collaboration. In a math lesson, groups might discuss solutions to a problem, and a randomly selected student presents the group's solution, reinforcing their understanding through peer discussion.

Quiz-Quiz-Trade promotes movement and active engagement, where students quiz each other with prepared questions and then trade cards to find a new partner. This structure involves each student holding a card with a question, quizzing a partner, trading cards, and repeating the process with a new partner. In a geography lesson, students might use cards with country names and capitals to quiz each other, enhancing their recall through repetition and varied questioning.

Implementation Strategies

Implementing Kagan Structures effectively requires clear instructions, modeling, active monitoring, and debriefing. Teachers should provide explicit instructions for each structure, ensuring students understand the process and expectations. Demonstrating how to perform the structure before asking students to participate can also enhance their confidence and competence.

Active monitoring during the activity is crucial, as teachers can circulate the room to listen in on discussions, providing guidance and ensuring all students are engaged. This support is particularly beneficial for students with Special Educational Needs (SEN), who might need additional encouragement to participate fully. After the activity, discussing what went well and what could be improved helps students reflect on their learning process and understand the value of the structure.

The benefits of Kagan Structures extend to fostering social skills, increasing confidence, and supporting diverse learning styles. By promoting equal participation and accountability, these structures create a dynamic and inclusive classroom environment. SEN students, in particular, benefit from the multiple entry points for participation and the supportive nature of peer interactions.

FRAYER MODELS

Using Frayer Models for Concept Development

The Frayer Model is a graphical organiser that enhances students' understanding of new concepts. It involves breaking down a concept into four sections: definition, characteristics, examples, and non-examples. This structured approach helps students thoroughly explore and internalise new vocabulary and ideas.

Structure and Benefits:

The Frayer Model consists of a central box that contains the concept or term being studied. Surrounding this central box are four sections:

In the Definition section, students write a clear and concise definition of the concept. This helps them understand the fundamental meaning of the term. The Characteristics section is where students list the essential features of the concept, helping them identify what makes the concept unique and recognisable. In the Examples section, students provide instances that illustrate the concept, reinforcing understanding by linking the concept to real-world or familiar cases. The Non-Examples section is for cases that do not fit the concept, helping students distinguish the concept from other similar or related ideas.

The benefits of using Frayer Models include promoting critical thinking, improving comprehension, and aiding retention. By organising information visually, students can better understand and remember new concepts. The model also encourages students to consider the broader context and relationships between ideas.

Practical Applications in the Classroom

Frayer Models can be integrated into various subjects and lessons to support concept development. They are particularly useful when introducing new vocabulary, complex ideas, or abstract concepts.

To use a Frayer Model effectively, begin by presenting the new concept or term to the class. Provide a brief overview and context to pique students' interest. Next, demonstrate how to complete a Frayer Model using a familiar term. Show students how to fill in each section with appropriate information.

Allow students to work in pairs or small groups to complete a Frayer Model for the new concept, providing guidance and support as needed. Bring the class together to discuss their completed models, encouraging students to share their definitions, characteristics, examples, and non-examples. This reinforces learning and allows for clarification of any misunderstandings. For independent practice, assign additional concepts for students to explore using Frayer Models, which helps solidify their understanding and encourages independent learning.

Examples and Best Practices

In a science lesson on photosynthesis, a Frayer Model could be used as follows. In the Definition section, students might write: "The process by which green plants use sunlight to synthesise food from carbon dioxide and water." The Characteristics section might include: "Involves chlorophyll, occurs in the chloroplasts, produces oxygen, requires sunlight." Examples in the Examples section could be: "Sunflower, oak tree, algae," while the Non-Examples section might list: "Human respiration, combustion, photosynthesis in animals."

In an English lesson on metaphors, the Definition section could include: "A figure of speech that involves comparing two unlike things directly without using 'like' or 'as.'" The Characteristics section might mention: "Implies similarity, used in literature and poetry, creates vivid imagery." Examples in the Examples section could be: "Time is a thief," "The world is a stage," while the Non-Examples section might list: "As brave as a lion," "Like a rolling stone" (similes).

In a history lesson on feudalism, the Definition section could state: "A social and economic system in medieval Europe where land was owned by lords and worked by serfs in exchange for protection." The Characteristics section might include: "Hierarchical structure, land-based economy, mutual obligations, decentralised power." Examples in the Examples section could be: "Medieval England, feudal Japan," while the Non-Examples section might list: "Modern democracy, capitalist economy."

Best practices for using Frayer Models include using clear and concise language to ensure definitions and characteristics are easily understandable. Encouraging collaboration by allowing students to work together on Frayer Models promotes discussion and deeper understanding. Incorporating visuals such as images or symbols can help visual learners and make the models more engaging. Regularly reviewing completed Frayer Models and reflecting on what has been learned reinforces retention and helps identify any areas needing further clarification.

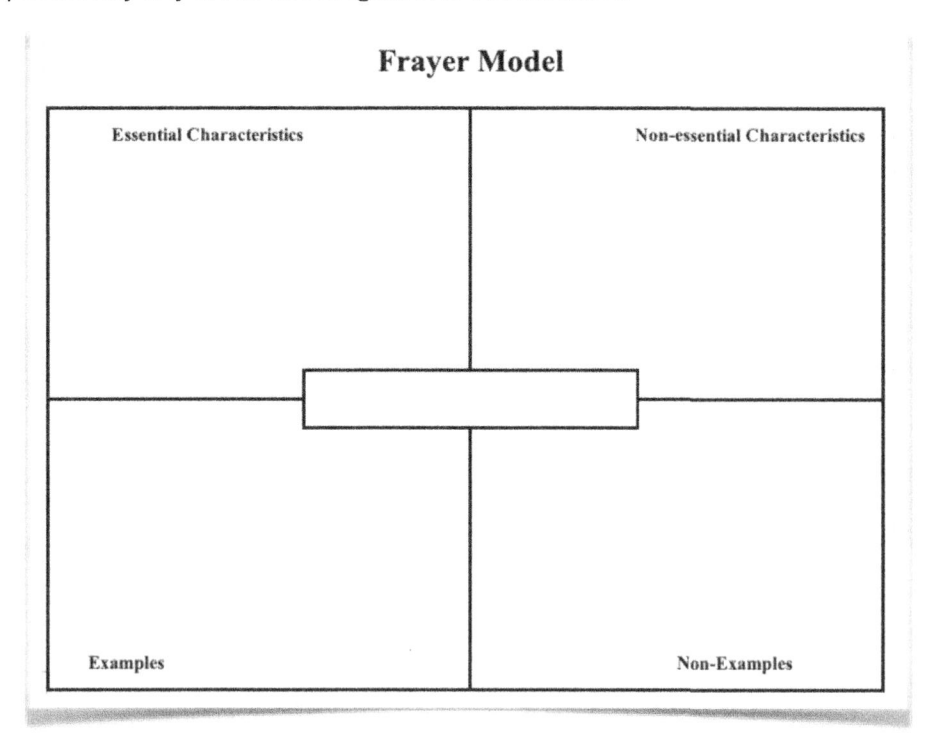

Frayer Model

Essential Characteristics	Non-essential Characteristics
Examples	Non-Examples

SENTENCE STARTERS

Providing Scaffolds for Student Responses

Sentence starters are an essential tool in the classroom, offering scaffolds that support students in constructing complete and coherent responses. They serve as prompts that help students begin their sentences, thereby easing the process of expressing their thoughts and ideas. Sentence starters are especially useful for students who struggle with language production, including those with Speech, Language and Communication Needs (SLCN) and those learning English as an Additional Language (EAL).

Importance of Sentence Starters

The importance of sentence starters lies in their ability to provide a structured way for students to articulate their responses. They help in guiding students 'thinking and ensure that their answers are complete and relevant to the question or discussion topic. By providing a starting point, sentence starters reduce the cognitive load on students, allowing them to focus more on the content of their response rather than on how to begin. This support is crucial for developing language skills, enhancing participation, and boosting confidence.

Sentence starters also promote inclusivity by enabling all students to participate in classroom discussions, regardless of their language proficiency. They encourage students to use academic language and complex sentence structures, which are essential for higher-order thinking and deeper understanding. Additionally, sentence starters can be tailored to various levels of difficulty, making them versatile tools for differentiated instruction.

Examples and Best Practices

Effective use of sentence starters involves providing a variety of prompts that cater to different types of responses. Here are some examples and best practices for incorporating sentence starters into classroom activities:

1. For Expressing Opinions:

    - "I believe that..."
    - "In my opinion..."

- "I think that..."

2. For Explaining Reasons:
    - "The reason for this is..."
    - "This happens because..."
    - "One explanation could be..."

3. For Making Predictions:
    - "I predict that..."
    - "I think that... will happen because..."
    - "Based on... I believe that..."

4. For Comparing and Contrasting:
    - "Similarly..."
    - "In contrast..."
    - "On the other hand..."

5. For Summarising Information:
    - "In summary..."
    - "To sum up..."
    - "In conclusion..."

Best practices for using sentence starters include modelling their use in your own speech and writing. Show students how to integrate these prompts into their responses by using them during class discussions and in written assignments. Encourage students to use sentence starters regularly by incorporating them into classroom activities and assignments. Display a list of commonly used sentence starters in the classroom as a reference for students. This can be done through posters, handouts, or a dedicated section on the classroom board.

Effective Use in Different Subjects

Sentence starters can be effectively used across various subjects to support student responses and enhance learning.

English: In English lessons, sentence starters can help students analyse texts, express their opinions about characters, or summarise plots. For example, when discussing a novel, a teacher might prompt students with, "The main character's motivation is..." or "A significant theme in this book is..."

Science: In science classes, sentence starters can aid in explaining scientific phenomena, formulating hypotheses, or drawing conclusions from experiments. For instance, after conducting an experiment, students could use starters like, "The results show that..." or "My hypothesis was correct because..."

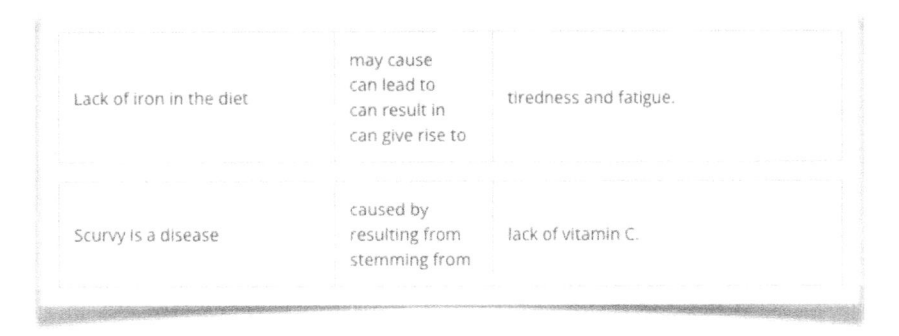

Lack of iron in the diet	may cause can lead to can result in can give rise to	tiredness and fatigue.
Scurvy is a disease	caused by resulting from stemming from	lack of vitamin C.

History: In history lessons, sentence starters can support students in discussing historical events, comparing different periods, or evaluating the impact of specific actions. Teachers might use prompts such as, "The key cause of this event was..." or "This event changed history by..."

In 1933, Three years later, From 1933 to 1945, In the 1930s and 1940s, During the Nazi period, Between 1933 and 1945,	restrictions were placed on German academics.

Maths: In maths, sentence starters can help students explain their problem-solving processes, describe patterns, or justify their answers. For example, students might use, "To solve this problem, I first..." or "The pattern I noticed is..."

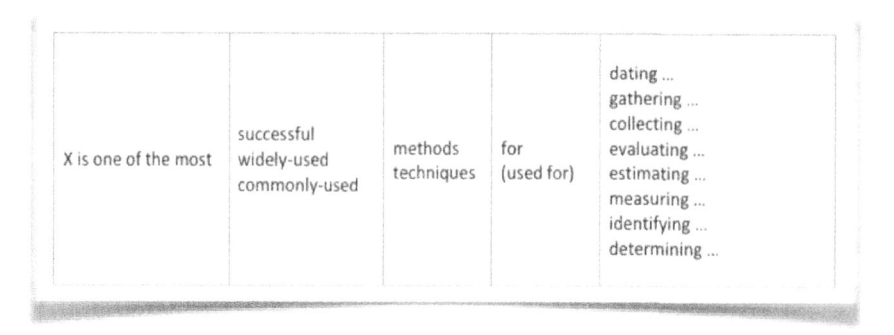

X is one of the most	successful widely-used commonly-used	methods techniques	for (used for)	dating ... gathering ... collecting ... evaluating ... estimating ... measuring ... identifying ... determining ...

Geography: In geography, sentence starters can assist students in explaining geographical processes, comparing different regions, or discussing human-environment interactions. Prompts like, "The climate in this region is..." or "Human activity has affected this area by..." can be useful.

Describing the process: sequence words

To begin this process, ...
The first step in this process was to ...
The second method used to identify X involved ...

Prior to	commencing the study, ethical clearance was sought from ... analysing the interview data, the transcripts were checked for ... undertaking the investigation, ethical clearance was obtained from ... data collection, the participants received an explanation of the project.
After	'training', the participants were told that ... collection, the samples were shipped back to X in ... testing for the presence of antibodies, the blood was ... the appliance was fitted, the patients attended X every four weeks.
On	arrival at the clinic, patients were asked to ... completion of X, the process of parameter estimation was carried out. obtaining written informed consent from the patients, a questionnaire was ...
Once	the samples were extracted, it was first necessary to ... the Xs were located and marked, a thin clear plastic ruler ... the positions had been decided upon, the Xs were removed from each Y and ... the exposures were completed, the X was removed from the Y and placed in ...
Following	correction for ..., X was reduced to ... conformational analysis of X, it was necessary to ... administration of X to patients, we assessed the effects on ... this treatment, the samples were recovered and stored overnight at ...

The participants were *then* shown a film individually and were asked to ...
The soil was *then* weighed again, and this weight was recorded as ...
These ratings were *then* made for the ten stimuli to which the subject had been exposed ...
The preparation was *then* placed in a custom-built microfluidics chamber, covered with ...

When	dividing X, care was taken to ... removing X, it was important to ... inviting the participants, the purpose of the research was clearly explained.

Finally, questions were asked as to the role of ...
In the follow-up phase of the study, participants were asked ...
The final stage of the study comprised a semi-structured interview with participants who ...

PROVIDING CONSTRUCTIVE FEEDBACK

Constructive feedback is essential for guiding student learning and improving performance. It provides students with clear, actionable insights into their strengths and areas for improvement, helping them understand how to advance their skills and knowledge.

Effective Feedback Methods

1. Specific and Timely Feedback
   Providing feedback that is specific and timely helps students understand exactly what they did well and what needs improvement. Immediate feedback is particularly effective as it allows students to correct mistakes and reinforce learning while the material is still fresh.

   Instead of saying, "Good job," specify what was done well: "Your analysis of the character's motivations was insightful because you used specific examples from the text."

2. Balanced Feedback
   Balanced feedback includes both positive comments and constructive criticism. Highlighting what students did well before addressing areas for improvement can help maintain their motivation and confidence.

   "Your essay had a strong introduction and well-structured arguments. To improve, you might add more evidence to support your main points in the body paragraphs."

3. Focused on Process and Effort
   Feedback that focuses on the process and effort rather than just the outcome encourages a growth mindset. This approach helps students understand that improvement comes from hard work and effective strategies.

   "I can see you put a lot of effort into solving this math problem. Next time, try breaking it down into smaller steps to avoid errors in calculation."

4. Actionable Suggestions
   Provide clear, actionable suggestions that students can implement to improve their work. This guidance helps them know exactly what steps to take next.

"To strengthen your conclusion, consider summarising your key points and suggesting a potential implication of your findings."

5. Interactive Feedback

   Engage students in the feedback process by asking questions and encouraging dialogue. This approach makes feedback a two-way communication, allowing students to reflect and ask for clarification.

   "You made a good point about the environmental impact of plastic. What other solutions can you think of to address this issue?"

Encouraging Student Reflection

Encouraging students to reflect on their learning and feedback helps them develop self-awareness and take ownership of their improvement process. Reflection promotes deeper understanding and personal growth.

1. Self-Assessment

   Encourage students to assess their own work before submitting it. Provide rubrics or checklists to help them identify strengths and areas for improvement.

   "Before turning in your essay, use this checklist to ensure you have a clear thesis, supporting evidence, and a strong conclusion."

2. Reflective Journals

   Have students keep reflective journals where they regularly write about what they learned, challenges they faced, and how they overcame them. This practice fosters ongoing self-reflection and personal growth.

   "Write a journal entry about what you found challenging in today's math lesson and how you plan to tackle similar problems in the future."

3. Peer Feedback

   Incorporate peer feedback sessions where students review and provide feedback on each other's work. This activity helps them learn to critique constructively and accept feedback from others.

   "Exchange essays with a classmate and provide feedback using the rubric. Focus on giving specific, actionable suggestions."

4. Goal Setting

   After receiving feedback, encourage students to set specific goals for improvement. This practice helps them focus on concrete steps they can take to enhance their learning.

> *"Based on the feedback you received, set one or two goals for your next assignment. Write down what you will do differently and how you plan to achieve these goals."*

5. Reflective Discussions

    Hold class discussions where students can share their reflections on feedback and learning experiences. This collaborative reflection helps build a supportive learning community.

    > *"Let's discuss what we learned from our latest project. What feedback did you find most helpful, and how will you use it to improve your work?"*

By integrating these strategies for providing constructive feedback and encouraging student reflection, teachers can create a classroom environment that supports continuous improvement and fosters a growth mindset. This approach not only enhances academic performance but also builds students' confidence and self-efficacy.

SUMMARISING KEY TECHNIQUES

We have explored several effective teaching strategies that enhance student learning and engagement through teacher talk. These techniques include:

- Simplification of Language: Using clear, straightforward language to reduce cognitive load and ensure that all students can access and understand instructional content. Simplifying language aligns with the principles of Universal Design for Learning (UDL) and is particularly beneficial in inclusive classrooms.

- Repetition: Repeating key information to reinforce learning and ensure retention. This method is crucial for embedding new concepts in students' long-term memory and is supported by cognitive science principles.

- Broken Record Technique: Repeating the same phrase or instruction consistently to help students focus and understand. This technique is especially helpful for students who need extra processing time, such as those with SLCN or EAL.

- Think-Pair-Share: An interactive strategy that enhances student engagement and learning through structured peer interaction. It involves individual thinking, paired discussions, and group sharing to promote deeper understanding and communication skills.

- Recasting: Subtly correcting and expanding students' responses by rephrasing them. This technique helps model correct language use and encourages more sophisticated thinking without directly pointing out errors.

- Frayer Models: A graphical organiser used to develop a deeper understanding of new concepts by breaking them down into definition, characteristics, examples, and non-examples. This method promotes critical thinking and retention.

- Sentence Starters: Providing scaffolds that help students begin their responses, supporting language development and ensuring coherent, complete answers. Sentence starters are useful across various subjects and enhance students' ability to articulate their thoughts.

Emphasising the Importance of Adaptation and Flexibility in Teaching

While these techniques are powerful tools for enhancing teaching and learning, their effectiveness depends on how well they are adapted to meet the unique needs of each classroom and student. Teachers must remain flexible and responsive, continuously assessing the impact of these strategies and adjusting their approaches as necessary.

Adapting techniques involves considering students' individual learning styles, language proficiencies, and any special educational needs. Flexibility in teaching means being prepared to modify lesson plans, provide additional support, and explore alternative methods to ensure that every student can succeed.

CHAPTER 3: QUESTIONING IN THE CLASSROOM

THE IMPORTANCE OF EFFECTIVE QUESTIONING

Questioning is one of the most powerful tools in a teacher's arsenal. When used effectively, questions can enhance student understanding, promote critical thinking, and encourage active participation. Questioning engages students in the learning process, helping them to explore ideas, clarify their thoughts, and deepen their comprehension of the subject matter.

Effective questioning goes beyond simply asking for facts; it involves probing students' understanding, challenging their assumptions, and encouraging them to make connections between different concepts. This type of questioning stimulates intellectual curiosity and motivates students to engage more deeply with the material.

Moreover, well-crafted questions can reveal students' thought processes and provide valuable insights into their learning needs. This allows teachers to tailor their instruction more effectively, addressing misconceptions and guiding students towards higher levels of thinking.

However, it is important to acknowledge that certain groups of students, such as those with Special Educational Needs (SEN) and those learning English as an Additional Language (EAL), may struggle with questioning. These students might find it difficult to process and respond to questions due to various challenges, including language barriers, cognitive processing issues, and anxiety.

SEN Students: Students with learning disabilities, attention deficits, or cognitive impairments may have difficulty understanding and responding to questions quickly. They might need additional time to process information and formulate their answers. Questions may need to be simplified or broken down into smaller, more manageable parts to support their understanding.

EAL Students: English language learners often struggle with questions due to limited vocabulary and language proficiency. They may not fully grasp the nuances of certain questions or might find it challenging to articulate their thoughts in English. Using visual aids, clear and simple language, and providing context can help these students understand and respond more effectively.

To support these students, teachers can employ strategies such as differentiated questioning techniques, scaffolding questions, and providing ample wait time. For more detailed strategies on how to adapt questions to support SEN and EAL students, please refer to the sections "Approaches to Questioning for SEN Students" and "Using Wait Time Effectively."

Mastering the art of questioning can transform classroom dynamics, making learning more interactive and inclusive. By fostering an environment where students feel comfortable to think critically and express their ideas, teachers can significantly enhance educational outcomes.

TYPES OF QUESTIONS: OPEN VS. CLOSED

Definitions and Differences

Understanding the types of questions teachers can use in the classroom is essential for fostering an environment conducive to learning and critical thinking. Open and closed questions serve different purposes and elicit different types of responses from students.

Closed Questions are those that can be answered with a single word or a short phrase. These questions typically focus on factual information, requiring students to recall or recognise data. For example, a teacher might ask, "What is the capital of France?" or "Did you complete your homework?" Closed questions are useful for checking factual understanding and for situations where a concise answer is needed.

Open Questions, on the other hand, require more elaborate responses and encourage students to think more deeply. These questions often start with words like "how," "why," or "what do you think about." For example, "How do you think climate change affects marine life?" or "Why do you believe the character acted this way?" Open questions stimulate discussion, critical thinking, and exploration of ideas, allowing students to express their thoughts and reasoning.

When to Use Open Questions

Open questions are particularly effective when the goal is to develop critical thinking skills, encourage discussion, and explore complex ideas. They are useful in various classroom situations:

- Promoting Deep Understanding: When teaching a new concept, open questions can help students make connections and understand the material on a deeper level. For instance, in a history lesson, asking "Why do you think this event was significant?" encourages students to think about the broader implications and causes.

- Encouraging Discussion: Open questions are excellent for stimulating classroom discussions. They allow students to share their opinions and listen to others, fostering a collaborative learning environment. For example, in an English class discussing a novel, asking "What do you think motivated the main character's actions?" can lead to a rich discussion.

* Assessing Higher-Order Thinking: These questions are aligned with higher levels of Bloom's Taxonomy, such as analysis, synthesis, and evaluation. For example, in a science class, asking "How would you design an experiment to test this hypothesis?" assesses students' ability to apply their knowledge and think critically.

When to Use Closed Questions

Closed questions are most effective when the goal is to assess specific knowledge, ensure understanding of key facts, or manage classroom activities efficiently. They are useful in the following scenarios:

* Checking for Understanding: After explaining a new concept, closed questions can quickly assess whether students grasp the basics. For example, "What is the formula for water?" ensures that students remember H_2O.

* Reviewing and Reinforcing Facts: Closed questions are useful for reviewing material and reinforcing factual knowledge. In a geography class, asking "Which continent is the largest?" helps students recall and reinforce their knowledge.

* Managing Classroom Behaviour: These questions can be used to quickly get students' attention or confirm completion of tasks. For example, "Did you bring your homework?" or "Are you ready for the next activity?" helps manage classroom routines efficiently.

Practical Application of Open and Closed Questions

Science Lesson on Ecosystems

In a Year 5 science lesson about ecosystems, the teacher begins by using closed questions to check prior knowledge:

- Teacher: "What is a producer in an ecosystem?"
- Student: "A plant."

Once the basic facts are established, the teacher shifts to open questions to deepen understanding:

- Teacher: "How do producers contribute to the energy flow in an ecosystem?"

- Student: "Producers, like plants, create their own food through photosynthesis, which provides energy for other organisms in the ecosystem."

English Lesson on Persuasive Writing

In a Year 7 English class focused on persuasive writing, the teacher uses closed questions to review key components:

- Teacher: "What is the purpose of a persuasive essay?"
- Student: "To convince the reader of a particular point of view."

To encourage critical thinking and discussion, the teacher then asks an open question:

- Teacher: "Why do you think using evidence is important in a persuasive essay?"
- Student: "Using evidence is important because it supports your arguments and makes them more convincing to the reader."

History Lesson on the Industrial Revolution

In a Year 8 history lesson, the teacher begins with closed questions to ensure students remember key facts:

- Teacher: "When did the Industrial Revolution begin?"
- Student: "In the late 18th century."

To promote deeper analysis, the teacher follows up with open questions:

- Teacher: "What were some of the social impacts of the Industrial Revolution?"
- Student: "It led to urbanisation, changed working conditions, and had significant effects on families and social structures."

Maths Lesson on Fractions

In a Year 4 maths class, the teacher uses closed questions to assess basic understanding:

- Teacher: "What is 1/2 plus 1/4?"

- Student: "3/4."

To challenge students and encourage problem-solving, the teacher asks an open question:

- Teacher: "How can you use fractions to explain why 1/2 is greater than 1/4?"

- Student: "If you divide a pizza into two parts, each part is bigger than if you divide it into four parts. So, 1/2 is more than 1/4."

BLOOM'S TAXONOMY AND QUESTIONING

Overview of Bloom's Taxonomy

Bloom's Taxonomy, developed by Benjamin Bloom and his colleagues in 1956, is a hierarchical model used to classify educational learning objectives into levels of complexity and specificity. It has been widely adopted in educational settings to help teachers structure their teaching and questioning techniques to promote higher-order thinking. The taxonomy consists of six levels, each representing a different type of cognitive process: Remembering, Understanding, Applying, Analysing, Evaluating, and Creating.

Level	Key Words
Evaluation (Evaluating)	Evaluate, Judge, Critique, Decide, Justify
Synthesis (Creating)	Create, Design, Develop, Formulate, Assemble
Analysis (Analysing)	Analyse, Differentiate, Organise, Formulate, Assemble
Application (Applying)	Use, Solve, Demonstrate, Apply, Construct
Comprehension (Understanding)	Explain, Summarise, Describe, Interpret, Compare
Knowledge (Remembering)	What, Who, When, Where, Which

The revised version of Bloom's Taxonomy, introduced by Anderson and Krathwohl in 2001, reorders the categories slightly and changes some of the terminology but retains the original concept's core principles. This revised taxonomy is often used today in educational settings, particularly for designing curriculum, assessments, and instructional strategies that foster comprehensive learning and critical thinking skills.

Applying Bloom's Taxonomy to Questioning

Applying Bloom's Taxonomy to questioning involves designing questions that correspond to each level of the taxonomy. This structured approach ensures that students are not only recalling information but also engaging in higher-order thinking processes, such as analysis, evaluation, and creation.

At the Remembering level, questions focus on recalling facts, definitions, and basic concepts. For example, a history teacher might ask, "What year did the Battle of Hastings occur?" This type of question assesses students' ability to remember essential details. Moving up to the Understanding level, questions require students to explain ideas or concepts in their own words. In a science class, a teacher might ask, "Can you describe the process of photosynthesis?" This ensures that students comprehend the material beyond mere memorisation.

At the Applying level, questions encourage students to use information in new situations. For instance, in a maths lesson, a teacher might ask, "How would you use the Pythagorean theorem to find the length of the hypotenuse in a right triangle?" This type of question helps students transfer their knowledge to practical problems. The Analysing level involves breaking down information into parts and examining relationships. A literature teacher might ask, "How does the author develop the theme of ambition in 'Macbeth'?" This prompts students to deconstruct the text and understand its underlying structure.

Evaluating questions require students to justify decisions or opinions. In a social studies class, a teacher might ask, "Do you think the policy implemented was effective? Why or why not?" This type of question encourages students to critically assess information and form reasoned arguments. Finally, at the Creating level, questions ask students to produce new or original work. An art teacher might ask, "Can you create a piece of artwork that represents the theme of resilience?" This type of question inspires students to synthesise their learning into creative expressions.

Encouraging Deeper Understanding for More and Most Able Students

For more and most able students and early finishers, it is crucial to encourage a deeper understanding of the material rather than simply repeating the same content at the same level or allowing them to 'move on' ahead of their peers. By engaging these students with higher-order questions and tasks that require more complex thinking, teachers can help them develop a richer and more nuanced understanding of the subject matter. For instance, students who quickly grasp the basic concepts of a topic can be challenged with analysing and evaluating scenarios related to the material, or they can be tasked with creative projects that require applying their knowledge in novel ways. This approach not only keeps advanced students engaged and motivated but also ensures that they are continuously challenged to think critically and deeply about what they are learning.

Examples of Questions at Different Levels

To effectively implement Bloom's Taxonomy in questioning, consider specific examples tailored to various subjects and contexts. In a history class, remembering-level questions might include, "What were the main causes of World War I?" Understanding-level questions could be, "Explain the significance of the Magna Carta." Applying-level questions might involve, "How would you apply the principles of the Magna Carta to modern-day laws?"

For analysing-level questions, a teacher might ask, "Analyse the impact of the Industrial Revolution on urban development." Evaluating-level questions could include, "Evaluate the success of the Treaty of Versailles in achieving lasting peace." Creating-level questions might prompt students to, "Design a utopian society based on the principles of equality and justice."

These examples illustrate how Bloom's Taxonomy can guide teachers in crafting questions that promote a range of cognitive skills, from basic recall to complex creation. By varying the levels of questioning, teachers can engage students more deeply and encourage comprehensive learning.

Using Bloom's Taxonomy in Questioning

Science Class

In a Year 7 science class learning about ecosystems, the teacher structures the lesson around Bloom's Taxonomy. The teacher begins with remembering-level questions such as, "List the different types of ecosystems." This establishes a foundation of basic knowledge. Moving to the understanding level, the teacher asks, "Explain how energy flows through an ecosystem," ensuring students grasp the concept.

Next, the teacher poses applying-level questions like, "Predict what would happen if a key species were removed from an ecosystem." This encourages students to use their knowledge in a hypothetical scenario. Analysing-level questions, such as, "Analyse the food web of a local ecosystem," prompt students to examine relationships within the system. Evaluating-level questions like, "Evaluate the impact of human activity on local ecosystems," require students to make judgments based on evidence. Finally, creating-level questions such as, "Design a sustainable ecosystem model," encourage students to synthesise their learning into a practical application.

English Literature Class

In a Year 9 English literature class studying Shakespeare's "Macbeth," the teacher uses Bloom's Taxonomy to guide questioning. The lesson begins with remembering-level questions, "Who are the main characters in 'Macbeth'?" to ensure students recall key details. Understanding-level questions follow, such as, "Summarise the plot of Act 1," helping students articulate the storyline.

Applying-level questions like, "Relate Macbeth's ambition to a real-life historical figure," encourage students to connect the text to broader contexts. Analysing-level questions, such as, "Analyse Lady Macbeth's role in Macbeth's downfall," prompt students to delve deeper into character motivations and plot development. Evaluating-level questions like, "Do you agree with Macbeth's actions? Why or why not?" engage students in critical thinking and moral reasoning. Finally, creating-level questions such as, "Write an alternative ending to 'Macbeth,'" inspire students to imagine new possibilities based on their understanding of the text.

By systematically incorporating questions from all levels of Bloom's Taxonomy, teachers can encourage deeper thinking and ensure a comprehensive understanding of the material. This approach not only supports the development of higher-order thinking skills but also makes learning more engaging and dynamic for students.

APPROACHES TO QUESTIONING FOR SEN STUDENTS

Questioning is a vital teaching strategy that fosters engagement, critical thinking, and deeper understanding. For students with Special Educational Needs (SEN), effective questioning techniques must be carefully crafted to meet their diverse needs and abilities. Effective questioning for SEN students involves understanding differentiation, tailoring questions to individual needs, and using scaffolding and visual aids to support learning. Through practical examples and real-world case studies, various methods for adapting questions for different abilities, implementing wait time effectively, and ensuring that all students have the opportunity to succeed in the classroom are demonstrated. Employing these strategies helps create an inclusive and supportive learning environment that promotes active participation and academic growth for SEN students.

Students with different Special Educational Needs (SEN) may face unique challenges when it comes to responding to questions in the classroom. Understanding these difficulties is crucial for teachers to adapt their questioning techniques effectively. Here are some examples:

Students with Autism (ASD/ASC)

Difficulties:

* Literal Interpretation: Students with ASD may interpret questions very literally and might struggle with abstract or hypothetical questions.

* Processing Time: They often need more time to process information and formulate responses.

* Social Communication: Difficulty in understanding social cues can make it challenging to engage in typical classroom questioning.

A teacher asks, "How would you feel if you were in the protagonist's situation?" A student with ASD might find it hard to imagine and articulate hypothetical emotions. Instead, the teacher could rephrase the question to, "What did the protagonist do in this situation, and why?"

Students with Dyslexia

Difficulties:

- Reading and Comprehension: They may struggle with reading the questions accurately and comprehending complex language.
- Processing Speed: Slower processing speed can make it hard to answer questions quickly.

For a student with dyslexia, a question like, "Summarise the main events of the story" can be challenging if they had difficulty reading the text. Providing questions orally and allowing extra time for responses can help.

Students with Attention Deficit Hyperactivity Disorder (ADHD)

Difficulties:

- Focus and Attention: Students with ADHD may find it difficult to stay focused on the question being asked.
- Impulsivity: They might blurt out answers without fully thinking them through.

A student with ADHD might struggle with a multi-part question like, "Explain the causes and effects of the Civil War." Breaking the question into smaller, more manageable parts and providing a structured outline can help maintain their focus.

Students with Anxiety

Difficulties:

- Being Put on the Spot: Students with anxiety may feel overwhelmed and unable to think clearly when asked to respond immediately.
- Fear of Making Mistakes: They may avoid answering questions due to a fear of being wrong or judged.

Instead of calling on a student with anxiety unexpectedly, a teacher could give them a heads-up by saying, "In a few minutes, I'll ask you to share your thoughts on this topic," allowing them time to prepare.

Students with Speech and Language Needs

Difficulties:

* Expressive Language: Difficulty in articulating thoughts and forming coherent responses.

* Vocabulary and Syntax: Limited vocabulary and challenges with grammar can hinder their ability to answer questions effectively.

A question like, "Describe the process of evaporation" can be difficult for a student with speech and language impairments. The teacher might provide sentence starters or visual aids to help them structure their response.

Students with Hearing Impairments

Difficulties:

* Hearing the Questions: Difficulty hearing the teacher or classmates clearly, especially in a noisy environment.

* Language Development: Delayed language development can impact their ability to understand and respond to questions.

For a student with a hearing impairment, a teacher should ensure they face the student while speaking and possibly use written questions or sign language. Visual aids and clear, concise language also support better understanding.

Students with Cognitive Needs

Difficulties:

* Cognitive Processing: Slower cognitive processing can make it challenging to understand and respond to questions quickly.

* Complexity of Questions: Difficulty with abstract thinking and complex questions.

A student with cognitive disabilities might find a question like, "Analyse the main character's motives in the story" too complex. Simplifying the question to, "What did the main character want to do?" and using concrete examples can aid their comprehension.

Understanding these difficulties and tailoring questioning techniques accordingly can significantly enhance the learning experience for SEN students, making the classroom more inclusive and supportive.

CHAPTER 4: QUESTIONING STRATEGIES

INTRODUCTION

Effective questioning is a powerful tool in the classroom, enhancing student engagement, critical thinking, and understanding. Questioning strategies are particularly important for supporting students with Special Educational Needs (SEN), ensuring that all learners can access and benefit from the curriculum.

Exploring differentiated questioning techniques helps teachers understand how to tailor questions to meet the diverse needs of their students. Assessing and adapting to individual student needs allows for questions that accommodate different abilities, providing practical examples across various subjects. Using visual aids and scaffolding questions supports students' understanding and confidence, enabling them to respond effectively.

Step-by-step questioning methods, which break down complex questions and gradually increase difficulty, help build student comprehension and confidence. The effective use of wait time is also crucial, giving students the necessary time to process and respond thoughtfully. Real-world case studies illustrate how these techniques can create a more inclusive and supportive learning environment.

By mastering these questioning strategies, teachers can foster a classroom atmosphere that encourages active participation, deeper understanding, and critical thinking, enabling all students to reach their full potential.

DIFFERENTIATED QUESTIONING TECHNIQUES

Understanding Differentiation

Differentiation is a teaching approach that involves tailoring instruction to meet the diverse needs of students. Rather than capping abilities or pre-determining who can achieve what, differentiation provides multiple pathways for all students to engage with and understand the material. This is particularly crucial in adaptive teaching, where the goal is to challenge students appropriately and foster growth.

In the context of questioning, differentiation means using various question types and techniques to engage students at their respective levels while promoting higher-order thinking. This approach ensures active participation from all students, including those with Special Educational Needs (SEN).

Strategies for Differentiated Questioning

1. Using a Range of Question Types
   Employing a mix of open-ended and closed questions allows teachers to cater to different cognitive levels. Open-ended questions encourage critical thinking and exploration, allowing students to elaborate on their thoughts. In contrast, closed questions can reinforce basic knowledge and provide a foundation for more complex inquiries.

   An open-ended question in an English lesson might be, "How do you think the protagonist felt after the main event in the story? Why?" This question prompts students to explore the character's emotions and motivations, fostering deeper engagement.

   A closed question might be, "What is the main event in the story?" This helps ensure that students have grasped the fundamental plot points.

2. Flexible Grouping
   Group students dynamically based on their needs and the specific learning objectives. Flexible grouping allows for varied peer interactions and targeted questioning. Mixed-ability groups can stimulate learning through peer support, while similar-ability groups allow for focused, level-appropriate questioning.

   In a science class, a mixed-ability group might discuss, "How does the ecosystem in the Amazon rainforest support various species?" Here, students learn from each other's insights and perspectives.

In a similar-ability group, the question might be, "List the key features of the Amazon rainforest ecosystem," allowing for more targeted discussions that build on their current understanding.

3. Scaffolded Questions

    Start with simpler questions and gradually increase complexity to build students' confidence and understanding. Scaffolding questions help all students progress from basic recall to higher-order thinking.

    Begin with a foundational question in a biology class: "What is photosynthesis?"

    Follow up with a more detailed question: "Why is photosynthesis important for plants?"

    Progress to a higher-order question: "How would life on Earth be different if plants could not perform photosynthesis?" This sequence allows students to build on their knowledge incrementally.

4. Using Visual Aids and Prompts

    Visual aids such as charts, diagrams, and pictures can help students understand and respond to questions. These aids are particularly beneficial for SEN students who may struggle with verbal explanations alone.

    In a geography lesson, a teacher might use a diagram of the water cycle and ask, "Look at this diagram of the water cycle. Can you explain what happens during evaporation?" The visual support helps students visualise the process and articulate their understanding.

5. Encouraging Think-Pair-Share

    Think-Pair-Share allows students to think about a question individually, discuss their thoughts with a partner, and then share with the larger group. This strategy promotes reflection, peer learning, and confidence in expressing ideas.

    In a history lesson, the teacher could prompt, "Think about a time when you worked on a team project. What made it successful? Share your thoughts with your partner, then we'll discuss as a class." This method engages students at multiple levels of processing and communication.

6. Providing Sentence Starters

    Sentence starters help students frame their responses, particularly those who may struggle with initiating answers. This support can be crucial for students with language processing difficulties.

> *During a literature discussion, a teacher might offer starters like, "One reason the character acted this way is because..." or "The main cause of the event was..." These prompts help students structure their thoughts and articulate their responses more effectively.*

7. Assessing and Adapting in Real-Time
Continuously assess student responses and adapt questions based on their needs. If a student answers a question easily, follow up with a more challenging question. If a student struggles, provide additional support or a simpler question to help them build their understanding.

> *In a PSHCE lesson, the teacher might start with, "What are the three branches of government?" If the student answers easily, the teacher could follow up with, "How do these branches interact with each other?" Conversely, if the student struggles, the teacher could ask, "Can you name one branch of government and its main function?"*

Differentiated questioning techniques are essential for creating an inclusive and effective learning environment. By understanding and implementing adaptive teaching strategies, teachers can challenge all students appropriately, encourage deeper understanding, and support the diverse needs of their classroom. This approach not only enhances student engagement but also fosters a growth mindset, ensuring that every student has the opportunity to succeed and thrive academically.

TAILORING QUESTIONS TO INDIVIDUAL NEEDS

Differentiation in questioning is not just about using various techniques; it also involves understanding the unique needs of each student and adapting questions accordingly. This approach ensures that every student is engaged and challenged appropriately, fostering an inclusive and supportive learning environment.

Assessing Student Needs

Effective differentiation begins with a thorough assessment of student needs. Understanding students' strengths, weaknesses, learning styles, and any specific challenges they face is crucial for tailoring questions that support their learning.

- Formal Assessments: Use standardised tests, quizzes, and other formal assessment tools to gauge students' knowledge and skills. This data provides a baseline understanding of where each student stands academically.

- Informal Assessments: Observe students during class activities, discussions, and interactions. Informal assessments such as exit tickets, classwork, and participation can offer insights into students' comprehension and engagement levels.

- Student Profiles: Develop comprehensive profiles for each student, incorporating information from assessments, previous academic records, and any Individual Education Plans (IEPs). These profiles help in understanding the specific needs and preferences of each student.

- Feedback and Self-Assessment: Encourage students to reflect on their own learning and provide feedback about what helps them understand better. This self-assessment can be invaluable in tailoring instruction to meet their needs.

Adapting Questions for Different Abilities

Once student needs are assessed, the next step is to adapt questions to match their abilities. This adaptation ensures that all students, regardless of their starting point, are challenged and supported appropriately.

- Varying Complexity: Adjust the complexity of questions based on the student's current level of understanding. For instance, a student who struggles with a concept might need basic recall questions, while another who excels might benefit from analysis or synthesis questions.

For a student struggling with the concept of democracy: "What is democracy?"

For a student who understands the basics: "How does democracy differ from other forms of government?"

- Scaffolding Questions: Provide scaffolding to help students build up to more complex questions. Start with simpler questions that lay the groundwork and gradually increase difficulty as the student's confidence and understanding grow.

    Initial: "What are the main parts of a plant?"

    Intermediate: "What role do roots play in a plant's life?"

    Advanced: "How do roots contribute to the overall health of an ecosystem?"

- Using Prompts and Hints: Offer prompts and hints to guide students towards the correct answer without giving it away. This method helps maintain student engagement and encourages independent thinking.

    Prompt: "Think about what happens when you water a plant. What part absorbs the water?"

- Providing Multiple Entry Points: Design questions that allow for multiple entry points, so students can respond at their level. This approach is particularly useful in mixed-ability classrooms.

    "Explain the water cycle in as much detail as you can." Students can respond based on their current level of understanding, from basic steps to more complex interactions.

Specific Techniques for Tailoring Questions

1. **Cold Calling**

   Cold calling involves selecting students to answer questions at random rather than only calling on those who volunteer. This technique ensures that all students are engaged and prepared to participate, but it needs to be applied thoughtfully.

   Student Anxiety: For students with anxiety, cold calling can be intimidating. Give them a heads-up or use less direct methods initially to build their confidence.

   Fairness and Inclusivity: Rotate among all students to ensure fair participation and avoid putting the same students on the spot repeatedly.

2. **Lolly Sticks**

   Using lolly sticks with students 'names written on them is another random selection method. This technique can be a fun and fair way to involve all students, but it should be adapted based on individual needs.

   Inclusion: Ensure that students with SEN are included and supported. For instance, pair lolly stick selection with prompts or scaffolds to help them prepare their responses.

3. **Hands Up/No Hands Up**

   The "hands up" approach allows students to volunteer, while "no hands up" encourages all students to be ready to answer. Balancing these methods can ensure active participation from all students.

   Encouraging Participation: For reluctant students or those with SEN, combine "no hands up" with supportive prompts or pair them with a peer for initial discussions before sharing with the class.

   Managing Dominant Voices: Ensure that more vocal students do not dominate discussions by setting clear expectations and rotating who gets to speak.

4. **No-Opt-Out**

   The no-opt-out strategy ensures that all students eventually provide an answer, even if they initially struggle. This technique helps build accountability and confidence.

Supportive Environment: Create a supportive atmosphere where students feel safe to make mistakes. Offer hints or rephrase the question to help struggling students arrive at an answer.

Gradual Implementation: Start with simpler questions to build confidence before moving to more challenging ones.

5. Say-It-Again-Say-It-Better

This technique involves asking students to repeat their answers with improvements or additional details. It encourages deeper thinking and clearer articulation.

Positive Reinforcement: Praise initial efforts and gently guide improvements. This approach can be particularly encouraging for students with language difficulties.

Scaffolding: Provide sentence starters or prompts to help students refine their answers.

6. Think-Pair-Share

Think-Pair-Share is a collaborative learning strategy where students first think about a question individually, then discuss their thoughts with a partner, and finally share their ideas with the larger group. This technique promotes reflection, peer learning, and confidence in expressing ideas.

Structured Interaction: Provide clear instructions and time limits for each phase (think, pair, share) to keep the activity focused and productive.

Support for SEN Students: Pairing students thoughtfully can ensure that those with SEN are supported and encouraged by their peers.

7. Wait Time

Wait time, or giving students a few moments to think before responding, can significantly enhance the quality of their answers. This strategy is particularly beneficial for students who need more time to process information.

Patience and Encouragement: Encourage all students to take their time and think through their answers. This helps create a low-pressure environment where thoughtful responses are valued over quick ones.

Implementation: After asking a question, count silently to five or ten before calling on a student to answer. This allows everyone a chance to think and prepares them to respond.

8. Socratic Questioning

    Socratic questioning involves asking a series of thought-provoking questions to stimulate critical thinking and illuminate ideas. This method encourages students to explore concepts deeply and articulate their reasoning.

    Guided Discovery: Use questions to guide students towards discovering answers themselves rather than providing direct explanations. This promotes independent thinking and deeper understanding.

    Flexibility: Be prepared to follow up with additional questions based on students' responses to keep the dialogue flowing and meaningful.

Tailoring Techniques to Specific Groups

Applying a blanket questioning policy in a diverse classroom can be ineffective and even detrimental. It's important to adapt these strategies based on individual student needs and characteristics.

Students with Anxiety:

- Cold Calling: Give these students a heads-up or allow them to pass and come back to them later.
- Think-Pair-Share: Use this method to build confidence in a smaller group before sharing with the class.

Students with SEN:

- Lolly Sticks: Pair with prompts or support to prepare responses.
- No-Opt-Out: Provide additional scaffolding or allow peer assistance.

More and Most Able Students:

- Say-It-Again-Say-It-Better: Challenge these students to refine their responses and provide more detailed explanations.
- Socratic Questioning: Engage them in deeper, more complex questioning to stimulate critical thinking.

Differentiated questioning techniques are essential for creating an inclusive and effective learning environment. By understanding and implementing adaptive teaching strategies, teachers can challenge all students appropriately, encourage deeper understanding, and support the diverse needs of their classroom. This approach not only enhances student engagement but also fosters a growth mindset, ensuring that every student has the opportunity to succeed and thrive academically.

SCAFFOLDING QUESTIONS FOR SEN STUDENTS

Importance of Scaffolding

Scaffolding is a crucial instructional strategy within adaptive teaching, especially for students with Special Educational Needs (SEN). The concept of scaffolding, introduced by Wood, Bruner, and Ross (1976), involves providing temporary support to students as they learn new concepts or skills. This support is gradually removed as students become more competent, promoting independent learning.

In the context of questioning, scaffolding helps bridge the gap between what students already know and what they need to learn. For SEN students, scaffolding questions can significantly enhance understanding, reduce anxiety, and build confidence. By breaking down complex questions into more manageable parts, teachers can guide students through the learning process, ensuring they comprehend each step before moving on.

Techniques for Effective Scaffolding

1. Breaking Down Complex Questions
   Complex questions can be overwhelming for SEN students. Breaking them down into smaller, more manageable parts helps students process information step by step.

   Original Question: "Explain how the water cycle works."

   Scaffolded Steps:

   a. "What happens when water evaporates from the surface of a lake?"
   b. "What do we call the process when water vapour turns into clouds?"
   c. "How does water return to the ground from the clouds?"

2. By addressing each part separately, students can build a complete understanding of the water cycle in stages.

3. Providing Prompts and Sentence Starters
   Prompts and sentence starters give students a framework for their responses, helping them structure their thoughts and articulate their answers more clearly.

Instead of asking, "Why do plants need sunlight?" provide the prompt: "Plants need sunlight because..."

For a more detailed question: "One reason plants need sunlight is because... Another reason is..."

4. Using Think-Alouds

    Think-alouds involve the teacher verbalising their thought process while working through a question or problem. This modeling helps students understand how to approach and solve similar questions.

    "Let's think about why leaves change color in the fall. First, we know that leaves get their green color from chlorophyll. When it gets colder, the chlorophyll breaks down, and we start to see other colors like red and yellow. So, why do leaves change color? Because the chlorophyll breaks down."

5. Providing Visual Aids

    Visual aids are powerful tools that can help scaffold questions for SEN students. They provide a visual representation of concepts, making them easier to understand and recall.

    Use a diagram of the water cycle while asking scaffolded questions. Point to each part of the diagram as you ask about evaporation, condensation, and precipitation.

Using Visual Aids

Visual aids support scaffolding by providing a concrete reference for abstract concepts. They can be particularly helpful for visual learners and students with language processing difficulties.

1. Diagrams and Charts

    Diagrams and charts can help students visualise relationships and processes, making complex information more accessible.

    A flowchart showing the steps of photosynthesis can be used to scaffold questions about the process. Start with "What is the first step in photosynthesis according to this chart?" and progress to "How does each step contribute to the plant's ability to produce food?"

2. Graphic Organisers

    Graphic organisers, such as Venn diagrams, mind maps, and T-charts, help students organise information visually, making it easier to compare and contrast ideas or outline processes.

When discussing the causes and effects of a historical event, use a cause-and-effect graphic organiser. Ask, "What were the causes of this event?" and fill in the organiser together, then move on to "What were the effects?"

3. Interactive Whiteboards and Digital Tools
Interactive whiteboards and digital tools can be used to create engaging visual aids that students can interact with directly. This interactivity can enhance understanding and retention.

Use an interactive whiteboard to display a timeline of events. Students can come up to the board and move events into the correct order as you scaffold questions about each event's significance.

Practical Examples of Scaffolding Questions

Science Lesson on Photosynthesis

Original Question: "Describe the process of photosynthesis."

Scaffolded Approach:

1. Show a diagram of a plant and ask, "What part of the plant absorbs sunlight?"
2. Provide a sentence starter: "The leaves absorb sunlight because…"
3. Use a flowchart of the photosynthesis process. Ask, "What happens to the sunlight once it is absorbed by the leaves?"
4. Guide with think-aloud: "The sunlight is used to convert carbon dioxide and water into glucose and oxygen. What do you think happens to the glucose?"

History Lesson on the Industrial Revolution

Original Question: "What were the main causes and effects of the Industrial Revolution?"

Scaffolded Approach:

1. Use a cause-and-effect graphic organiser. Start with, "What were some of the inventions during the Industrial Revolution?"

2. Prompt with a sentence starter: "One important invention was... because..."
3. Show a timeline of the Industrial Revolution. Ask, "How did these inventions change the way people worked?"
4. Guide with think-aloud: "The invention of machinery made production faster and cheaper. What effect did this have on workers?"

By employing these scaffolding techniques and incorporating visual aids, teachers can effectively support SEN students in understanding and responding to questions. This adaptive approach ensures that all students are engaged, confident, and able to progress in their learning.

USING WAIT TIME EFFECTIVELY

Importance of Wait Time

Wait time, also known as think time, refers to the pause a teacher gives students after asking a question and before expecting a response. Research by Mary Budd Rowe (1972) indicates that extending wait time to at least 3-5 seconds can significantly enhance the quality and depth of student responses. For students with Special Educational Needs (SEN), who may require more time to process information and formulate answers, the value of wait time cannot be overstated. It promotes an inclusive classroom environment where all students have the opportunity to participate and engage in higher-order thinking.

Strategies for Implementing Wait Time

1. Silent Counting
   After posing a question, count silently to at least five before calling on a student to answer. This practice ensures that all students, including those who need more processing time, have a fair chance to think about their response.

Ask, "What are the causes of the water cycle?" Then silently count to five before selecting a student to answer.

2. Non-Verbal Cues
   Use non-verbal cues, such as holding up your hand or making eye contact, to signal that you are waiting for a response. This can encourage students to think more deeply without feeling rushed.

Pose the question, "How does photosynthesis benefit the environment?" and then make eye contact with the class, indicating that you expect thoughtful responses.

3. Prompting Reflection
   Encourage students to take their time and reflect on their answers. Verbal prompts can remind students that it is okay to think before they speak.

Say, "Take a moment to think about how the protagonist's actions influenced the plot. I'll give you a few seconds."

4. Pair and Share
   Incorporate think-pair-share activities where students first think individually about the question, then discuss their thoughts with a partner before sharing with the class. This method builds in wait time and allows students to refine their ideas through discussion.

Ask, "Why is democracy important in society?" Have students think silently, then discuss with a partner, and finally share with the class.

5. Written Responses
   Provide opportunities for students to write down their thoughts before responding orally. This strategy can be particularly effective for students who need more time to organise their ideas.

Pose the question, "What are the main themes in the novel?" Give students a minute to jot down their thoughts before discussing.

6. Wait Time with Follow-Up
   Use wait time not only before the initial response but also after a student's answer to encourage further elaboration and deeper thinking.

After a student answers, "Photosynthesis helps plants make food," pause again and then ask, "Can you explain why this process is crucial for the entire ecosystem?"

In the classroom

Science Class
Question: "What role does gravity play in the solar system?"

Strategy: After asking, silently count to five. If no one answers, prompt with, "Think about how planets stay in orbit around the sun."

Maths Class
Question: "How can we solve this quadratic equation?"

Strategy: Pose the question, wait for five seconds, then use a non-verbal cue like pointing to the equation on the board to encourage responses.

History Class
Question: "What were the main causes of World War I?"

Strategy: Ask the question, give students a moment to write their thoughts, then discuss in pairs before sharing with the class.

By effectively implementing wait time, teachers can enhance student participation, promote deeper thinking, and create an inclusive classroom environment that supports all learners, particularly those with SEN. This strategy not only improves the quality of student responses but also fosters a more thoughtful and reflective learning atmosphere.

ENHANCING ENGAGEMENT THROUGH QUESTIONING

Encouraging Student Participation

Questioning is a powerful tool in the classroom, not only for assessing knowledge but also for engaging students and fostering a dynamic learning environment. The Socratic method, which involves asking and answering questions to stimulate critical thinking and illuminate ideas, is one of the oldest and most effective forms of engagement through questioning. Research has consistently shown that active participation in learning, facilitated by effective questioning, leads to deeper understanding and better retention of information (Chi, 2009).

Effective questioning techniques encourage all students to participate, which is crucial for creating an inclusive classroom. When students are actively engaged, they are more likely to be invested in their learning, take ownership of their educational journey, and develop critical thinking skills. The act of responding to questions helps students to articulate their thoughts, process information, and connect new knowledge to existing understanding.

Creating an Inclusive Environment

Creating an inclusive environment through questioning involves recognising and addressing the diverse needs of students. Inclusive questioning strategies ensure that all students, regardless of their abilities or backgrounds, have the opportunity to contribute. This is particularly important for students with Special Educational Needs (SEN), who may require different approaches to feel comfortable and confident in participating.

Research by Vygotsky (1978) on the Zone of Proximal Development (ZPD) highlights the importance of social interaction in learning. According to Vygotsky, students learn best when they are challenged just beyond their current abilities and supported through interaction with more knowledgeable others, including teachers and peers. Effective questioning places students within their ZPD, providing the right level of challenge while supporting their learning process.

Building Confidence in Answering Questions

Building confidence in students when it comes to answering questions is crucial for engagement. Students are more likely to participate if they feel confident in their ability to contribute meaningfully. This confidence can be fostered through a supportive classroom environment and consistent positive reinforcement.

Strategies to Build Confidence:

- Use Encouraging Language: Reinforce the idea that all contributions are valuable. Avoid negative feedback that might discourage future participation.

- Provide Scaffolding: Support students with prompts and hints to help them arrive at an answer. This builds their confidence and competence over time.

- Celebrate Effort: Acknowledge the effort students put into thinking and responding, not just the accuracy of their answers.

Supporting Reluctant Responders

Reluctant responders are students who are hesitant or unwilling to participate in classroom discussions. Identifying and engaging these students is essential for creating an inclusive and dynamic learning environment. Understanding the reasons behind their reluctance, whether it be anxiety, lack of confidence, or previous negative experiences, is the first step in addressing their needs.

Identifying Reluctant Responders:

- Observation: Pay attention to students who consistently avoid eye contact, fidget, or show signs of discomfort when questions are asked.

- Self-Reports: Encourage students to share their feelings about participating in class discussions through anonymous surveys or one-on-one conversations.

Strategies for Engaging Reluctant Responders:

- Tailored Approaches: Use individualised strategies to engage reluctant responders, such as giving them advance notice of questions or allowing them to discuss answers with a peer before sharing with the class.

- Positive Reinforcement: Provide positive feedback to build their confidence. Recognise their efforts and contributions to encourage further participation.

- Safe Environment: Create a classroom atmosphere where mistakes are viewed as learning opportunities rather than failures. This helps reduce the fear of being wrong.

A student with anxiety is given the option to discuss their answer with a partner before sharing it with the class. This reduces the pressure and builds confidence.

A reluctant responder is praised for their effort, regardless of the accuracy of their answer. This positive reinforcement encourages them to participate more in future discussions.

ASSESSMENT AND FEEDBACK THROUGH QUESTIONING

Effective questioning is not only a tool for engaging students but also a powerful means of assessing their understanding and providing constructive feedback. Formative assessment through questioning allows teachers to gather real-time insights into student learning, identify areas of confusion, and adapt instruction accordingly. This dynamic approach helps create a responsive and supportive classroom environment where teaching is tailored to meet the needs of all students.

Questioning as an assessment tool enables ongoing evaluation of student progress. By asking targeted questions, teachers can gauge comprehension, diagnose misconceptions, and measure cognitive skills. This immediate feedback loop is essential for guiding instructional decisions and ensuring that learning objectives are being met.

Providing constructive feedback through questioning encourages student reflection and self-assessment. When students are given thoughtful, specific feedback on their responses, they gain a clearer understanding of their strengths and areas for improvement. This process not only enhances learning but also fosters a growth mindset, where students view challenges as opportunities for development.

Using questions to inform teaching practice involves analysing student responses to identify trends and adjust teaching strategies. By reflecting on the effectiveness of their questions and the quality of student answers, teachers can refine their approach to better support student learning.

Formative Assessment Techniques

Formative assessment through questioning is an essential strategy for gauging student understanding and guiding instruction in real-time. Unlike summative assessments, which evaluate learning at the end of an instructional period, formative assessments provide continuous feedback that can inform teaching and learning throughout the process.

1. Diagnostic Questions
   Diagnostic questions help identify students' prior knowledge and misconceptions at the beginning of a lesson or unit. These questions are

designed to uncover students' understanding and pinpoint areas that need clarification.

In a science lesson on ecosystems, ask, "What do you know about food chains?" This question assesses students' baseline knowledge and reveals any misconceptions.

2. Probing Questions
   Probing questions delve deeper into students' initial responses, encouraging them to expand on their answers and think critically. These questions help teachers assess the depth of student understanding.

   If a student answers, "Photosynthesis is how plants make food," follow up with, "Can you explain why sunlight is important in this process?" This probes the student's comprehension of the underlying mechanisms.

3. Reflective Questions
   Reflective questions encourage students to think about their learning process and self-assess their understanding. These questions can be used at the end of a lesson to promote metacognition.

   After a history lesson on World War I, ask, "What was the most surprising thing you learned today, and why?" This encourages students to reflect on their learning and articulate their thoughts.

4. Socratic Questioning
   Socratic questioning involves asking a series of thoughtful, open-ended questions that lead students to discover answers through dialogue and reasoning. This technique fosters critical thinking and deeper understanding.

   In a literature class discussing a novel, ask, "What motives might the protagonist have for their actions?" followed by, "How do these motives affect the story's outcome?"

Adapting Instruction Based on Responses

Adapting instruction based on student responses is a key component of effective formative assessment. By listening to and analysing students' answers, teachers can adjust their teaching strategies to address gaps in understanding and reinforce key concepts.

1. Identifying Misconceptions

   Pay close attention to student responses to identify common misconceptions. Address these misconceptions immediately to prevent them from becoming entrenched.

   If several students incorrectly explain a scientific concept, such as the phases of the moon, pause the lesson to revisit the basic principles and clarify misunderstandings.

2. Providing Immediate Feedback

   Use student responses to provide immediate, specific feedback. This helps students understand what they did well and where they need improvement.

   If a student correctly explains a math problem but makes a minor error in calculation, acknowledge their understanding of the process while guiding them to correct the mistake: "You've set up the equation correctly, but let's take another look at this step."

3. Differentiating Instruction

   Based on the diversity of student responses, differentiate instruction to meet the varied needs of the classroom. Group students for targeted instruction, provide additional resources, or adjust the complexity of tasks.

   For students who quickly grasp a concept, provide extension activities that challenge their thinking. For those who struggle, offer additional practice or one-on-one support.

4. Using Exit Tickets

   Exit tickets are brief assessments given at the end of a lesson to gauge student understanding. They provide valuable feedback that can inform the next day's instruction.

   After a geography lesson, ask students to write down one thing they learned and one question they still have. Use their responses to plan targeted review or extension activities for the next class.

5. Iterative Questioning

   Continuously ask questions throughout the lesson to monitor understanding and adjust instruction dynamically. This ongoing assessment helps ensure that all students are following along and grasping key concepts.

During a discussion on the water cycle, periodically ask questions like, "What happens after evaporation?" and "How does precipitation contribute to the water cycle?" Adjust the pace and depth of instruction based on student answers.

Using questions for formative assessment and adapting instruction based on student responses are vital strategies for effective teaching. These techniques ensure that learning is responsive and tailored to the needs of all students, fostering a dynamic and inclusive classroom environment. By continuously assessing and adjusting their teaching methods, educators can enhance student engagement, understanding, and achievement.

SUMMARISING KEY TECHNIQUES IN QUESTIONING

We have explored several effective questioning strategies that enhance student engagement, critical thinking, and understanding in the classroom. These techniques include:

Formative Assessment Techniques: Using diagnostic, probing, reflective, and Socratic questioning to gauge student understanding and guide instruction in real-time. This approach helps identify misconceptions, promote deeper thinking, and provide immediate feedback to support learning.

Types of Questions: Open vs. Closed: Employing a mix of open-ended and closed questions to cater to different cognitive levels and teaching objectives. Open questions stimulate critical thinking and discussion, while closed questions assess specific knowledge and manage classroom activities efficiently.

Bloom's Taxonomy and Questioning: Applying Bloom's Taxonomy to structure questions that promote higher-order thinking. This involves crafting questions that encourage students to remember, understand, apply, analyse, evaluate, and create, ensuring comprehensive learning.

Differentiated Questioning Techniques: Tailoring questions to meet the diverse needs of students by varying complexity, using flexible grouping, and providing scaffolding. This adaptive approach ensures that all students, including those with Special Educational Needs (SEN), are challenged appropriately and supported in their learning.

Scaffolding Questions for SEN Students: Breaking down complex questions, using prompts and sentence starters, and incorporating visual aids to support SEN students. This method helps bridge gaps in understanding and build confidence.

Using Wait Time Effectively: Implementing wait time to enhance the quality of student responses. Giving students the necessary time to process information and formulate answers fosters a more inclusive and thoughtful learning environment.

Enhancing Engagement through Questioning: Encouraging student participation and creating an inclusive environment by using questioning techniques that build confidence and support reluctant responders. Strategies such as think-pair-share, positive reinforcement, and creating a safe space for mistakes are crucial for engaging all students.

Assessment and Feedback through Questioning: Using questioning as a tool for ongoing assessment and feedback. Analysing student responses helps adjust teaching strategies, provide constructive feedback, and encourage student reflection and self-assessment.

Emphasising the Importance of Adaptation and Flexibility in Teaching

While these questioning techniques are powerful tools for enhancing teaching and learning, their effectiveness depends on how well they are adapted to meet the unique needs of each classroom and student. Teachers must remain flexible and responsive, continuously assessing the impact of these strategies and adjusting their approaches as necessary.

Adapting questioning techniques involves considering students' individual learning styles, language proficiencies, and any special educational needs. Flexibility in teaching means being prepared to modify lesson plans, provide additional support, and explore alternative methods to ensure that every student can succeed.

By mastering and thoughtfully applying these questioning strategies, teachers can create a more interactive, adaptive, and effective learning environment. This approach not only enhances student engagement and understanding but also fosters a growth mindset, ensuring that every student has the opportunity to succeed and thrive academically.

About the Author

Abigail Hawkins – The Driving Force Behind Inclusive Education

With over 30 years of experience, Abigail Hawkins stands as a seasoned and passionate SENCO, renowned for her commitment to advancing Special Educational Needs (SEN) provisions. As the founder of SENDCO Solutions and SENsible SENCO CIC, Abigail leverages her extensive expertise to offer invaluable support and guidance to educators and schools nationwide.

A Champion for All Learners

Abigail's vast experience spans a diverse range of subjects, addressing the needs of students from toddlers to adults. Her practical approach to SEN issues is underscored by a wealth of consultancy work, where she collaborates with leading software and product companies to pioneer innovative tools for SEN support. Her efforts extend to designing and delivering teaching assistant apprenticeship and master's degree programs, as well as authoring several books and resources on SEN and exclusions. Additionally, Abigail provides comprehensive support to schools through detailed reviews, targeted training sessions, and ongoing consultancy to ensure the effective implementation of SEN strategies.

Leading a Thriving Network

As the founder of a support network that empowers nearly 13,000 SENCOs, Abigail is dedicated to fostering connections and sharing vital resources. Her impactful tenure as the Chair of Governors for three schools in the East Midlands highlights her unwavering commitment to educational leadership.

Pioneering Beyond Traditional Channels

Abigail's influence transcends traditional educational frameworks. During the challenging lockdown periods, she was a key figure in hosting a series of SEN webinars that reached a global audience exceeding 60,000 viewers. Embracing modern communication methods, she also manages a successful YouTube channel, making SEN-related information both accessible and engaging.

A Relentless Advocate for Inclusive Education

Abigail's non-nonsense, hands-on approach enables her to make a significant impact in the lives of countless students, educators, and schools. Her steadfast dedication to inclusive education remains evident through her continuous efforts to promote and implement effective SEN strategies.

Becoming a subscriber to SENsible SENCo offers a wealth of advantages designed to support and enhance your role as an SEN professional. As a member, you will gain:

- **Exclusive Access to Resources**: Unlock a treasure trove of expertly curated materials, including guides, templates, and best practice strategies tailored specifically for SEN coordinators and educators.

- **Cutting-Edge Insights**: Stay ahead with the latest developments in SEN research, policy updates, and innovative teaching methods through our regularly updated content and newsletters.

- **Professional Development**: Benefit from comprehensive training modules, webinars, and workshops that provide valuable CPD opportunities, helping you to refine your skills and knowledge.

- **Community Support**: Join a vibrant community of like-minded professionals, sharing experiences, advice, and support through our forums and networking events.

These QFT booklets have been distributed to subscribers as an online version and they can easily access the videos that accompany.

www.sensiblesenco.org.uk

Printed in Great Britain
by Amazon